MESSAGE OF THE FATHERS OF THE CHURCH

General Editor: Thomas Halton

Volume 2

MESSAGE OF THE FATHERS OF THE CHURCH

JESUS, CHRIST & SAVIOR

by

Gerard H. Ettlinger, SJ

Michael Glazier
Wilmington, Delaware

About the Author

GERARD H. ETTLINGER, SJ, holds a doctorate in patristic theology from Oxford University. He is currently Professor of Patristics at Fordham University. Among his publications are critical editions of Greek texts by John Chrysostom and Theodoret of Cyrus.

First published in 1987 by Michael Glazier, Inc.
1935 West Fourth Street, Wilmington, Delaware 19805.

Distributed outside U.S., Canada, Australia, and Philippines by Geoffrey Chapman, a division of Cassell Publishers Ltd., Artillery House, Artillery Row, London SW1P 1RT.

Library of Congress Catalog Card Number: 86-46355
International Standard Book Number:
  Message of the Fathers of the Church series:
    (0-89453-312-6, Paper; 0-89453-340-1, Cloth)
JESUS, CHRIST & SAVIOR
  (0-89453-314-2, Paper)
  (0-89453-342-8, Cloth)

Cover design: Lillian Brulc

Typography by S. Almeida

Printed in the United States of America.

Table of Contents

Editor's Introduction

The *Message of the Fathers of the Church* is a companion series to The *Old Testament Message* and The *New Testament Message*. It was conceived and planned in the belief that Scripture and Tradition worked hand in hand in the formation of the thought, life and worship of the primitive Church. Such a series, it was felt, would be a most effective way of opening up what has become virtually a closed book to present-day readers, and might serve to stimulate a revival in interest in Patristic studies in step with the recent, gratifying resurgence in Scriptural studies.

The term "Fathers" is usually reserved for Christian writers marked by orthodoxy of doctrine, holiness of life, ecclesiastical approval and antiquity. "Antiquity" is generally understood to include writers down to Gregory the Great (+604) or Isidore of Seville (+636) in the West, and John Damascene (+749) in the East. In the present series, however, greater elasticity has been encouraged, and quotations from writers not noted for orthodoxy will sometimes be included in order to illustrate the evolution of the Message on particular doctrinal matters. Likewise, writers later than the mid-eighth century will sometimes be used to illustrate the continuity of tradition on matters like sacramental theology or liturgical practice.

An earnest attempt was made to select collaborators on a broad inter-displinary and inter-confessional basis, the chief consideration being to match scholars who could handle the Fathers in their original languages with subjects in which they had already demonstrated a special interest and competence. About the only editorial directive given to the selected contributors was that the Fathers, for the most part, should be allowed to speak for themselves and that they should speak in readable, reliable modern English. Volumes on individual themes were considered more suitable than volumes devoted to individual Fathers, each theme, hopefully, contributing an important segment to the total mosaic of the Early Church, one, holy, catholic and apostolic. Each volume has an introductory essay outlining the historical and theological development of the theme, with the body of the work mainly occupied with liberal citations from the Fathers in modern English translation and a minimum of linking commentary. Short lists of Suggested Further Reading are included; but dense, scholarly footnotes were actively discouraged on the pragmatic grounds that such scholarly shorthand has other outlets and tends to lose all but the most relentlessly esoteric reader in a semi-popular series.

At the outset of his *Against Heresies* Irenaeus of Lyons warns his readers "not to expect from me any display of rhetoric, which I have never learned, or any excellence of composition, which I have never practised, or any beauty or persuasiveness of style, to which I make no pretensions." Similarly, modest disclaimers can be found in many of the Greek and Latin Fathers and all too often, unfortunately, they have been taken at their word by any uninterested world. In fact, however, they were often highly educated products of the best rhetorical schools of their day in the Roman Empire, and what they have to say is often as much a lesson in literary and cultural, as well as in spiritual, edification.

St. Augustine, in *The City of God* (19.7), has interesting reflections on the need for a common language in an expanding world community; without a common language a man is more at home with his dog than with a foreigner as far as intercommunication goes, even in the Roman Empire, which imposes on the nations it conquers the yoke of both law and language with a resultant abundance of interpreters. It is hoped that in the present world of continuing language barriers the contributors to this series will prove opportune interpreters of the perennial Christian message.

Thomas Halton

Acknowledgements

I wish to express my gratitude to Fordham University for granting me a Faculty Fellowship and a leave of absence, which gave me the time to complete this volume.

I owe a special word of thanks to my Jesuit Community at Fordham University for its support during my time away from the university.

Most of all, I would like to thank the Brothers of the Sacred Heart at Monsignor McClancy High School in Queens, New York, with whom I have served as chaplain during the composition of this volume. The kindness with which they shared their religious community with me, together with their support and encouragement, have provided me with an atmosphere of peace that facilitated my academic endeavors.

Abbreviations

ACO	Acta Conciliorum Oecumenicorum, ed. E. Schwartz
CCL	Corpus Christianorum, series latina (Turnhout)
CSEL	Corpus Scriptorum Ecclesiasticorum Latinorum (Vienna)
GCS	Die griechischen christlichen Schriftsteller der ersten drei Jahrhunderte (Berlin)
Jaeger	Gregorii Nysseni Opera, ed. W. Jaeger et al (E.J. Brill)
Loeb	The Loeb Classical Library (Cambridge, Mass.)
OECT	Oxford Early Christian Texts (Oxford)
PG	Patrologia graeca, ed. J.P. Migne
PL	Patrologia latina, ed. J.P. Migne
SC	Sources Chrétiennes (Paris)
ST	Studi e Testi (Vatican City)

Introduction

I. Christ and Savior

"But who do you say that I am?" According to the author of Matthew's gospel, Jesus posed this question to his disciples, and Peter's response won for him a pre-eminent position among his peers and in the organization known as the church of Christ which developed out of that group.[1] The source of this church's life and activity is, of course, Jesus Christ, and the possibility of union with God through his saving work depends on the ability of each believer to answer well the question which Christ asked his disciples.

As one reads the writings of those members of the early church who are called its fathers, it becomes clear that their response to Christ's question rested on a faith which was grounded in the Christian scriptures, for they often cited texts from both testaments, with certain texts being used over and over again by almost every author. And yet, although they had, in scripture, a common source for their teaching on Christ and his saving work, they expressed their beliefs in an often bewildering variety of forms. As individuals, they came from widely disparate social, cultural, and

[1] Mt. 16.15-19.

educational backgrounds, and their personal motivations and aspirations were as different as the pressures imposed on them from outside by the needs of the people with whom they worked.

Their answers to Jesus's question were, accordingly, framed in a variety of theological and philosophical constructs, as well as in forms which have little or no conceptual content. In other words, some did not go beyond the practical answers of faith, simply stating their understanding of scripture's teaching about who Jesus was and what he did, and seeking to make this meaningful to themselves and to their audience. Others, however, preferred to put their faith under a microscope, as it were, in an attempt to show that Christians are intelligent human beings, submitting rationally in faith to the claims of this person, Jesus Christ.

One of the most striking characteristics of early Christian teaching about Christ and salvation is, therefore, its diversity. Although, even in the earliest period, certain ideas were condemned as totally aberrant, and, therefore, non-Christian,[2] the spectrum of orthodoxy, or correct thought, was a broad one. Some today would attribute this diversity to confusion, or to a lack of development or sophistication; and yet, this is the very same historical period that is characterized as a time of great fervor and faith, and one that is often considered to be normative for Christianity. The true explanation of this phenomenon probably lies in a combination of some, or all of these factors, but they must be viewed positively, and not as signs of deficiency. Thus the faith experience of the early believers led to an understanding of Christ and salvation which was, if not highly developed, still quite complex; since there was no central authority that could impose universal forms of thought or expression, absolute uniformity was never achieved. If homogeneity is considered an ultimate ideal, then the early church does leave much to be desired. But if diversity is a reflection, in human expe-

---

[2]Such ideas were branded as unorthodox or heretical.

rience, of the infinite richness of God, then it can be considered, in fact, a sign of wisdom.

Despite the pluralistic nature of early Christian expression of faith in Christ, there is a common object of belief which is expressed in the title of this book, *Jesus: Christ and Savior.* According to Christian faith, a person named Jesus, born in a particular time and place, was in fact the savior promised in the Old Testament, the Christ, or anointed one, who was sent from God to save human beings. His early followers clearly believed that this Jesus was more than a human being,[3] and they considered him capable of performing a task which no ordinary person could do: saving human beings from the power of sin and death by reestablishing a true relationship between them and God. The one object of Christian faith is, therefore, Jesus the Christ, human being, God, and savior. This relatively simple statement summarises the basic content of early Christian faith in Christ, and all who professed to be Christian would, in general, agree on it. The diversity and pluralism discussed above enter the scene, when attempts are made, as already indicated, to explain what this material means and how it affects the believer.

The writers of the early church saw that, when answering the question which Jesus posed, one must not separate the person from his work. And so, opponents of the Arian heresy in the early fourth century, for example, argue for the savior's divinity from the salvation which he effects. The controversies which ended in the general councils of Ephesus (431) and Chalcedon (451) were concerned primarily with the person of Christ—they attempted to explain who Christ was and how such a person could actually exist. But the confession of faith approved at the latter meeting preserved

---

[3]This is indicated in the titles which are applied to him in the writings known as the New Testament. Two are of special interest: "Son of God," which, in its literal sense, is self-explanatory, and "lord." The latter title was used in his own religious tradition as a substitute for the name of the God who made and sustains all things, but whose name the people did not dare to utter; "lord" is, then, simply another word for "God."

the accent on salvation which can be found in every public declaration of faith beginning with the first general council of Nicaea (325): "for us and for our salvation."

The overwhelming concentration on a quasi-philosophical discussion of the person and natures of Jesus Christ during the late fourth and early fifth centuries overshadowed the importance of his saving work, and future generations began to look at the theology of the Savior's person (Christology) as an area of concentration totally distinct from that of the saving work (Soteriology). In the beginning, however, it was not so, and the "message of the fathers" is that Jesus Christ was a real human being who was also truly God; this person was the savior of humanity, for, by suffering, dying, and rising from the dead, he put an end to the power which the devil, sin, and death had over humanity because of the sin of Adam and Eve. He created humanity anew, and he made it possible for all human beings to be united with God.

There were also writers in the early church who drew a different picture of Jesus the Christ. Some thought that he was indeed God, but not truly human; his human activity, therefore, was viewed as a kind of puppet show, designed to appeal to the human senses. Salvation in this system had nothing to do with Christ's human activity, but was rather a question of the believer's piercing the externals to reach the hidden spiritual reality. Others went to the opposite extreme and found him to be a good man, who had a special relationship with God; according to this view union with God would be achieved through faith in this man, whose good life earned for him resurrection from the dead, which would be a reward for his followers as well. He is thus called a son of God, but is not truly God. These extreme views were ultimately rejected on the ground that they suppressed one or more aspects of the mystery that was Christ and his saving work, and were not, therefore, authentically Christian. Since that rejection is supported by most of the early Christian writers, such opinions are not represented in this volume.

II. Methodology

1. GENERAL PRINCIPLES

Introductory comments will be kept brief, in order to allow the early Christian authors to speak for themselves; the material that is provided is intended to point out the directions in which their thought develops, and to give an indication of the major controversies and official reactions to them. The basis on which particular texts were chosen will be explained in the following section.

All the selections in this volume have been newly translated from the original languages when possible. The texts cited are not all translated in full; extraneous material has been omitted, but to avoid endless repetition of dots and dashes such omissions have not been indicated. Book, chapter, and section listings are normally printed at the end of each item; the system used for enumerating individual quotations should be clear, although it varies somewhat because of the way in which ancient texts have been divided. Words enclosed in square brackets [sic] are not actually in the text, but have been supplied to complete the sense. Proper names and the words God and Christ will be capitalized. Father, Son, Spirit, and Word will also be capitalized, when they clearly refer to a member of the Christian trinity.

Scriptural passages have been translated anew from the texts of the early Christian authors used here, since they often quote the bible from memory and do not offer a standard version; scriptural references will follow the system used in the *Oxford Annotated Bible*; where the Septugint version differs from the Hebrew text on which the *OAB* is based, both references will be listed, and the Septuagint version will be marked "LXX"; the same practice will be followed for Latin authors who have used a Latin text based on the Septuagint rather than on the Hebrew.

2. GENERAL NORMS FOR SELECTION OF TEXTS

Since the contents of this anthology are largely determined by the scope of the series to which it belongs, it has
resulted in a work that is different from already existing
volumes on the same topic. Among existing anthologies a
collection edited by Richard Norris deals specifically with
the so-called Christological controversy and is, therefore,
restricted to narrowly defined areas of "Christology."[4] A
volume in "The Library of Christian Classics" deals only
with "Christology" from the fourth century on.[5] An older
work, *Word and Redeemer*, does quote the earliest authors
and touches on the issue of salvation; but it is chiefly concerned with tracing the teaching of the council of Chalcedon
(451) through each stage of the tradition, and is, as a result,
rather tendentious and flawed.[6] Finally, two volumes edited
and translated by Henry Bettenson cite authors from all
periods on both Christ and salvation; but the two issues are
treated separately, since the quotations, which are brief and
intended to highlight the major points, are arranged according to themes.[7]

This anthology, as noted above, will treat the person and
work of Christ as two realities inseparably joined, so that
many selections will deal with both "topics" at the same
time. It begins with the earliest post-apostolic writers and
ends in the middle of the fifth century, with the council of
Chalcedon forming, as it were, a watershed of the early
Christian view of Christ and salvation. It does not deal
directly with the major trinitarian and christological controversies, but attempts to go behind them to the expression
of the church's faith, which was the context in which those

[4]*The Christological Controversy*, Richard A. Norris, Jr. (translator/editor);
Sources of Early Christian Thought. Philadelphia: Fortress Press, 1980.

[5]*Christology of the Later Fathers*, Edward R. Hardy (editor); Philadelphia:
The Westminster Press, 1954 (first edition).

[6]James M. Carmody, S.J. and Thomas E. Clarke, S.J. (editors); Glen Rock,
N.J.: Paulist Press, 1965.

[7]*The Early Christian Fathers*, Oxford University Press, 1956, and *The Later
Christian Fathers*, Oxford University Press, 1970.

controversies arose. The majority of the selections have been taken, therefore, not from official or polemical documents, but from homilies, letters, and more informal treatises, where writers tended to present their personal beliefs, and which thus provide a more accurate record of the "message of the fathers." No attempt has been made to select passages which are in total harmony with the teaching of the council of Chalcedon or with any other "official" statement of church teaching, for the pluralism described in the first part of this introduction was characteristic of Christian thought throughout the whole period covered here. All the authors cited, with a few possible exceptions,[8] were considered orthodox, mainstream writers, and their teaching can be taken as representative of the Christian faith of their time. Although many of the passages quoted here will not be found in other collections, there is some unavoidable overlap with items in the works mentioned above, since certain texts are so crucial that they cannot be omitted.

III. Early Christian Texts and Modern Issues

According to the writers of the early church, scripture teaches that God wishes all human beings to be saved and for that reason entered into human existence. Their message is, therefore, particularly relevant to several significant areas of modern theology, for they believed that salvation through Jesus Christ was effected when God became human and liberated all human beings from the enslaving power of Satan, sin, and death. Since this evil power involves injustice and suffering, early Christian thought on Christ and salvation does touch upon the root insight of liberation theology.

Since salvation is thought by the early church to be dependent on the Christ's being both true God and a true

---

[8] Origen, Tertullian, Theodore of Mopsuestia, and Theodoret of Cyrus; comments on their status will be made in the appropriate chapters.

human being, with all that this latter term implies,[9] some comments are in order here on the relationship between the contents of this volume and the current debate on the role of women in the Christian church. Two factors in the early church's teaching on Christ and salvation must be noted: God became human in Jesus Christ, and the salvation he offered was available to all human beings. Salvation is not, therefore, limited by considerations of sex, age, color, ethnic derivation, or any other specifically human characteristic. The first of these factors is a source of extensive discussion in the modern church.

While Jesus was, in fact, a male who lived in a certain place at a specific time in history, it is clear that, for the early church, his humanity was the determining factor in salvation, not his maleness. Historically, this distinction has not always been made, so that, in the Roman Catholic church, for example, the maleness of Jesus Christ has been proposed as a reason for excluding women from the priesthood, which actualizes the salvation that Christ is and brings. Since the nature of priesthood and the offering of sacrifice are intimately linked with the person and saving work of Jesus Christ, the early church's thought on one area should shed light on the other as well.

Although no serious orthodox thinker in the early or contemporary church would in principle exclude women from at least passive participation in the saving work of Christ, statements which are anti-female can be found in the early tradition. Even today, as noted above, women are barred from an active role in making that salvation available to others. It may be possible to explain the existence of this negative attitude through socio-historical, linguistic, philosophical, and even religious or theological factors, but it does exist, and it cannot be ignored, since it is part of the Christian tradition. At the same time, it is clear that such material does not represent the whole Christian tradition,

[9]As the readings will show, the early church believed that Jesus Christ was exactly like all other human beings, with the sole exception that he had never sinned.

and may even be a deviation, found in many orthodox writers, from the principles of mainstream Christianity, which were expressed by a relatively small number of equally orthodox authors.

A number of the texts selected for this volume show that the person and work of Jesus Christ are directed to all human beings and are not limited by his maleness. Such texts are rarely, if ever, quoted in anthologies of "Christology" and/or "Soteriology," since they are considered peripheral at best to these two "areas" of Christian thought. It should be clear from all that has been said, however, that, when Christ's person and work are considered together, as they are in this collection, statements relating to the maleness of Jesus Christ and the role of women in the church are indeed significant.

Human language externalizes thought, which in turn is an expression of reality, either as it actually is, or at least as the thinker perceives it to be. In speaking about God, Christ, and salvation, then, one must strive to avoid language that would distort or limit the universality of God's saving will and of the saving work of Jesus Christ. One of the most striking examples in English of a problem in this area is the traditional version of the creed of Nicaea and Constantinople, in which one reads that God "became man...for us men and for our salvation." While some would argue that, linguistically, the word "man" in cases like this includes human beings of both sexes, there are others who disagree; they would maintain that such language is the product of a basically patriarchal society and religious tradition, in which men play the dominant roles and one speaks of God only in the masculine gender. If the second position is correct, then this kind of language would reflect a male bias and could be called sexist; whatever the case, however, such English usage is a misrepresentation of the meaning of the original Greek text, and this volume shall attempt to address that situation.

The English word "man" in the credal citation above stands for the Greek word anthropos, whose primary meaning is "human being." In this book that word will be translated by one of the following terms: human being, human, person, or human person; when it modifies another noun, it will sometimes be rendered as an adjective meaning human. Finally, since the early writers often used a concrete term to express an abstract idea, it will at times be translated as humanity. The term "son of man" presents a special problem, since it has become a consecrated phrase in scriptural translations; it will be retained here in that form, but it should be understood in light of the preceding discussion, and the complex development of its meaning must be taken into consideration.

It should be stressed that these comments do not suggest that an original text is to be translated arbitrarily, or in a way that would distort its author's intent. When a writer clearly refers to God or a member of the Christian trinity as a male figure, the masculine forms will be retained; this will be especially true when the reference is to God as Father or Son. On many occasions, however, even though the masculine form of a pronoun is found in the original, this does not necessarily mean that the writer views the person spoken of as a male.

A passage written by Arnobius, a fourth century Latin writer, dealing with a different issue, shows that this problem was not unknown in the early church.[10] Writing against classical Roman religion, which offered a pantheon of male and female deities indulging in various forms of sexual activity, Arnobius says that, even though Christians use the masculine gender in speaking of their deity, they do not believe that the God whom they worship is male. According to Arnobius, Christians do not believe that deities have bodies, and so there can be no male or female in God. But many of the words referring to God are masculine in gender, he says, and therefore, require the masculine forms of words that are in grammatical agreement with them.

In Greek, the words for God (*theos*) and Word (*logos*) are both masculine; in Latin, God (*deus*) is masculine, but Word

[10] *Adversus Nationes*, III.8, CSEL 4.116.

(*verbum*) is neuter; Spirit is neuter in Greek (*pneuma*), but masculine in Latin (*spiritus*). It may be useful to note that the word for God's Wisdom, an Old Testament image that was sometimes equated in the early period with God's Word or with God's Spirit, is feminine in both Greek (*sophia*) and Latin (*sapientia*), as well as in Hebrew, and was often personified as a female. The translations in this volume assume that the gender of pronouns in the original text are determined by that of the nouns to which they refer, unless the imagery is clearly male, as in the case of God the Father and God the Son.

Christian theology throughout its history has taught that God is a spirit, who, therefore, transcends human categories, including, of course, that of sex. This spiritual God entered history to save all human beings, and to that end became a human being, Jesus Christ; although he was a male, therefore, the salvation which he brought and brings flows from his humanity, not from his maleness. One may, then, conclude that, in mainstream Christian tradition, the attribution of sex to God is either symbolic or the result of word usage that requires gender distinctions.

This volume will not, therefore, alter ancient texts to satisfy the sensibility of the present age. It does, however, attempt to avoid erroneous translations that distort the tradition, and, in light of the foregoing discussion, it seeks to call attention, within that tradition, to a linguistic and conceptual bias that stems from the fundamentally patriarchal nature of the society and the religion in which early Christianity arose and developed.

Chapter 1

The Earliest
Post-Scriptural Writers

I. Introduction

The earliest post-scriptural Christian writers were not concerned with philosophical discussions about the personal nature and activity of the Christ. They were, for the most part, leaders and teachers in local churches, trying to explain to recently converted believers the way in which their faith was to be lived. Salvation meant union with God, the maker of all things, and one attained this goal through faith in Jesus the Christ. The main focus, then, was on God as the source and the goal of human life; the Christ was the mediator, whose role was absolutely essential, but who remained in a very real sense subordinate to the creator. Their relationship was not always clearly expressed; the images of God and God's Word or of Father and Son were most often used, and the Christ is even at times identified with God's Spirit.

The picture of the Christ at this time is usually based on a rather literal reading of the Jewish scriptures, the extant Pauline literature, and the material which would later be included in the New Testament canon as the gospels. Jesus was, therefore, viewed as the fulfillment of God's promises to the chosen people; he is the one sent by God, the servant of God, the Son of God, the messiah and savior. The true meaning of these titles and images and the possibility of their being realized in one person are not questioned or even discussed; they are taken for granted as data of revelation. This savior is generally depicted as fulfilling two functions, which are, in fact, not really distinct from one another. The Christ is, first of all, a *revealer*, who shows God to believers and brings God's truth to them. This revelatory function achieves its fruition through the saving work (i.e., the salutary effects of his life, death, and resurrection) of Christ as *redeemer*.

One of the earliest documents of post-biblical Christian literature is a letter from the church of Rome to the church of Corinth; it has come to us under the name of Clement, one of the earliest leaders (bishops) of the Roman Christian community. The letter stresses the unity and harmony which Christians should share as their heritage from Jesus the Christ, who came from God to lead believers to God.

Ignatius, bishop of Antioch in Syria, was traditionally believed to have died early in the second century; troubled by his emphasis on the central role of the bishop in the church, however, some scholars have, in recent years, attempted to date him a century or more later. But this new chronology has not been universally accepted, since his stress on the bishop's function may simply flow from his view of Christ and salvation. We know Ignatius through letters he wrote to local churches which he visited while being taken from Antioch to Rome, where he was to be put to death for his faith; the letters clearly envisage the bishop as a representative of Christ on earth and a summation in one person of the entire Christian community. But the important part of this image, for Ignatius, is not the bishop, but Christ, whom Ignatius believes to be truly divine and truly human, and, as such, able to offer salvation to believers. It may be anachronistic, therefore, to see in the role of Ignatius's bishop the hierarchical or monarchical episcopate which developed in later centuries. The fact is that, while union with God is, for Ignatius as for Clement, the goal of Christian life, the former stresses the role of the Christ (and therefore of the bishop who represents Christ) far more than does Clement. Ignatius's language about the Christ is perhaps even more striking for his day than what he says about the episcopacy.

As noted earlier, the writings of this period often display a vagueness in their understanding of the person and function of Jesus the Christ. This is significant, for it indicates that the early Christian conception of the savior was not based simply on a monolithic revelation received clearly at a given point in time, but was rather the result of development over a period of centuries. A striking example of this phenomenon is the *Didache* (or *Teaching*) *of the Twelve Apostles*, a second century disciplinary manual containing first century elements, which is not quoted here; its context is Jewish Christian, and Jesus is mentioned only briefly, although he is called "lord" and "Son" of God. The so called *Letter of Barnabas* is a second century treatise that is structured like the *Didache*; its Christianity is based more on opposition to the Old Testament than on a positive faith in Christ. The author affirms that Jesus is the Christ promised in the Old Testament, but spends more time rejecting the latter's ability to give salvation than in explaining the work of Christ.

Some early documents draw pictures of the Christ which were received from mainstream Christianity, but which were influenced by concepts that were later rejected. A second century homily which was for years considered to be a second letter of (the perfectly orthodox) Clement of Rome to the Corinthians is certainly not authentic, for it sketches a Christ who is so spiritualized as to be almost purely symbolic and not human.

Still other works, such as the *Shepherd of Hermas,* which, like the *Didache*, was considered almost as canonical scripture in the second century, show so little interest in Christ as God and Savior that the few formulations to be found there are either bizarre or erroneous, at least by later standards. Hermas never mentions the name of Jesus. Much of his thought is presented in the literary fiction of a dialogue between a lay preacher named Hermas and various figures of heavenly origin who reveal God's message to him. The first selection is traditional, but vague; the others, in which the Son of God seems to be identified with the Spirit, speak for themselves.

II. The Writings

1. ROME TO THE CORINTHIANS (THE LETTER OF CLEMENT)

1. Let us gaze intently at the blood of the Christ and realize that it is precious to God his Father, since it was shed for our salvation and brought the grace of repentance to the whole world. (7.4)[1]

2. This, my beloved, is the path through which we have discovered our salvation, Jesus Christ, who is the high priest of our offerings, and who protects us and helps our weakness. Through him we gaze at the heavenly heights; through him we see, as in a mirror, the perfect and exalted face of God; through him the eyes of our hearts were opened; through him our ignorant and darkened understanding springs up toward the light; through him the lord wished us to taste immortal knowledge. (36.1-2)[2]

3. The apostles preached to us the gospel they received from the lord Jesus Christ; Jesus the Christ was sent from God. The Christ, therefore, was from God, and the apostles were from the Christ; both, then, were set in proper order by God's will. (42.1-2)[3]

4. The master received us in love; because of the love which he had for us, our lord Jesus Christ, through God's will, gave his blood for us, his flesh for our flesh, and his soul for our souls. (49.6)[4]

[1] Text: *The Apostolic Fathers,* Loeb, I, 18-20.

[2] Text: *The Apostolic Fathers,* Loeb, I, 70.

[3] Text: *The Apostolic Fathers,* Loeb, I, 78-80.

[4] Text: *The Apostolic Fathers,* Loeb, I, 92-94.

2. IGNATIUS OF ANTIOCH

To the Trallians[5]

1. Do not listen, therefore, when someone speaks to you apart from Jesus Christ, who was descended from David and from Mary; he was truly born, and he truly ate and drank; he was truly persecuted under Pontius Pilate, was truly crucified and died, in the sight of those in heaven, on earth, and under the earth. He was also truly raised from the dead; his Father raised him, in the same way that his Father, through Jesus Christ, will raise those of us who believe in him, without whom we do not have the true life.(9)

To the Philadelphians[6]

2. I believe in the grace of Jesus Christ, who will break all your chains, and I encourage you to act as Christian disciples, not according to party lines. I heard people saying, "If I do not find it in the records, I do not believe in the gospel message"; when I replied to them, "It is written down," they answered me, "That is the question." As far as I am concerned, Jesus Christ is the record; the holy records are his cross and death, his resurrection, and faith through him; through these, with your prayers, I wish to be justified. The priests were good, but better is the high priest who was entrusted with the holy of holies, and to whom alone the mysteries of God were committed; he is the door to the Father, through which enter Abraham, Isaac, Jacob, the prophets, the apostles, and the church—all these enter into God's unity. But the gospel message has something special: the appearance of the savior, our lord Jesus Christ, his suffering and resurrection. (8-9)

[5] Text: *The Apostolic Fathers,* Loeb, I, 220.
[6] Text: *The Apostolic Fathers,* Loeb, I, 246-248.

To the Ephesians[7]

3. Ignatius, known also as the bearer of God, sends the warmest greetings in Christ Jesus and with perfect joy to the church, deservedly called blessed, which is in Ephesus of Asia—a church that was blessed with greatness through the fullness of God the Father, and was predestined from eternity to exist forever without change, united and chosen in true suffering, through the will of the Father and of Jesus Christ, our God. (Greeting)

4. In God I welcomed that beloved name of yours, earned through your natural righteousness, in accordance with faith and love in Christ Jesus, our savior. Imitating God and inflamed by the blood of God, you accomplished your common task perfectly. Since love does not permit me to be silent about you, I have taken it upon myself to exhort you to live in harmony with God's mind. For Jesus Christ, the life that is forever ours, is the Father's will, just as the bishops, appointed through the whole world, are in the will of Jesus Christ. (1 and 3)

5. It is, therefore, right for you to live in unity with the mind of the bishop. For your elders, who deserve this name and are worthy of God, are united to the bishop, as strings are fitted to a lyre. Through your unity and your harmonious love, therefore, Jesus Christ is sung. Form yourselves, then, into a choir, so that, in harmony and accord, you may take the keynote of God in unity and sing with one voice through Jesus Christ to the Father, so that he may hear you and realize, because of your good works, that you are members of his Son. It is to your advantage, therefore, to live in perfect unity, so as to share always in God. (4)

6. If I, in a short time, developed with your bishop an intimacy which is not merely human, but spiritual, how heartily, then, do I congratulate you, who have been joined to him, as the church is to Jesus Christ, and as Jesus Christ is to the Father, so that everything might be in harmonious unity. Let no one be deceived; if one is not within the sanc-

[7]Text: *The Apostolic Fathers,* Loeb, I, 172-196.

tuary, one is deprived of the bread of God. For if the prayer of one or two has such power, how much stronger is the prayer of the bishop and the whole church. Whoever avoids the common assembly, therefore, is already showing pride, and has severed relations with it. It is written, "God resists the proud"; let us be careful, then, not to resist the bishop, so that we might remain obedient to God. (5)

7. The more one sees that the bishop keeps silent, the greater respect one should have for him; for we should receive anyone whom the master sends to manage his household, just as we would receive the very one who sent him. It is clear, therefore, that we must regard the bishop as the lord himself. Onesimus praises highly your orderly conduct in God, because you all live according to the truth, and because no heresy finds its home among you. You do not even listen to people, unless they speak about Jesus Christ with truth. (6)

8. There are people who go about wearing the name in an evil and deceitful way, while acting in a manner that is unworthy of God; you must avoid them like wild beasts, for they are mad dogs who bite without your realizing it. You must watch out for them, for they are hard to cure. There is one doctor, both fleshly and spiritual, begotten and unbegotten, God in human form, true life in death, from both Mary and God, first able to suffer and then unable to do so, Jesus Christ our lord. (7)

9. People of the flesh cannot do works of the spirit, any more than people of the spirit can do works of the flesh, just as faith cannot do works of infidelity, and infidelity cannot do those of faith. But even the works you do according to the flesh are spiritual, for you do everything in Jesus Christ. (8)

10. I have learned that certain outsiders passed through your area bringing bad teaching, but that you did not permit them to sow the seed among you; you closed your ears to avoid receiving what they sowed, since you are stones of the Father's temple, prepared for a building of God the Father, lifted up to the top by the crane of Jesus Christ, the cross,

and using the Holy Spirit as a rope. Your faith is what draws you up, and love is the road that brings you up to God. And so you are all travellers on the same journey, carrying with you God, the temple, Christ, and holiness, adorned in every way with the commandments of Jesus Christ. (9)

11. Through our gentleness let us be seen as other people's brothers, and let us strive to imitate the lord, anxious not to be outdone in suffering injustice and deprivation, and in being despised. Thus no plant of the devil will be found among you, but you will abide in perfect purity and moderation through Jesus Christ, both in the flesh and in the spirit. (10)

12. These are the last days. Let us, therefore, live reverently, and let us fear God's patience, so that it does not turn into judgement against us. Let us either fear the wrath to come or love the grace at hand, making the choice only in order to be found with Christ Jesus in eternal life. Let nothing seem good to you apart from him, through whom I carry about my chains, the spiritual pearls with which I hope to rise again through the help of your prayers, in which I trust I shall always share. In this way I shall appear as part of the inheritance of the Ephesian Christians, who have always been one with the apostles through the power of Jesus Christ. (11)

13. You know all this, if you have, for Jesus Christ, perfect faith and love, which are the beginning and end of life. Faith is a beginning, love is an end, and God is the two of them joined in unity; everything else that leads to goodness follows after them. No one who professes faith sins, and no one who has acquired love hates. "The tree is known from its fruit" (see Mt. 12.33); in the same way people who claim to belong to Christ will be recognized through their actions. (14)

14. It is better to be silent and to be what one professes than to speak and to be false. Teaching is good, if the speaker also acts. There is one teacher, then, who spoke and it was done (see Ps. 33.9 [LXX, 32.9]); and what he did, even in silence, is worthy of the Father. One who has truly acquired the word of Jesus can also hear his silence, so as to

be perfect; thus he may act through what he says and be known through his silence. Nothing escapes the lord, and even our secrets are close to him. Let us do everything, therefore, as though he were dwelling within us, so that we might be his temples and that he might be our God within us (see I Cor. 3.16). (15)

15. Do not be deceived; corrupters of homes shall not inherit God's kingdom (see I Cor. 6.9 and Eph. 5.5). If, then, those who do this according to the flesh have died, how much worse is it to corrupt with bad teaching the faith for which Jesus Christ was crucified. A person like this is foul and will go into the unquenchable fire, as will anyone who pays attention to him. This is why the lord accepted oint-ment on his head (see Jn. 12.3): to breathe immortality on the church. Do not be anointed with the foul smelling teach-ing of the prince of this world, lest he take you captive from the life that is set before you. Why do we not all become prudent when we have received the knowledge of God which is Jesus Christ? Why do we die in our foolishness without recognizing the gift which the lord has truly sent to us? (16-17)

16. My spirit is a devoted servant of the cross, which is a stumbling block to unbelievers (see I Cor. 1.23 and Gal. 5.11), but salvation and eternal life to us. "Where are the wise? Where is the debater?" (I Cor. 1.20). Where is the boasting of those who are called prudent? Our God, Jesus the Christ, was conceived by Mary, according to God's plan, from the seed of David and the Holy Spirit (see Rom. 1.3). He was born and was baptized, in order to purify the water by suffering. (18)

17. Mary's virginity and her childbearing, as well as the lord's death, were kept hidden from the prince of this world—three mysteries of proclamation which were carried out with God's silence. How, then, was he revealed to the world? A star brighter than all stars shone in the sky; its light was inexpressible and its newness produced amazement. All the other stars, together with the sun and the moon, joined as a choir around this star, but it surpassed them all with its

radiance, and confusion arose as to the source of this new reality unlike the others. As a result, all magic was dissolved, every bond of evil disappeared, ignorance was destroyed, the old kingdom fell into ruin, for God appeared in human form to bring the new reality of eternal life (see Rom. 6.4), and what God had prepared now took its beginning. And so all things were disturbed, because plans were being made for the destruction of death. (19)

18. If, through your prayers, Jesus Christ judges us worthy, and if it is his will, in the second work which I plan to write to you, I shall clarify the discussion that I have started here about the dispensation of the new human being Jesus Christ, [which is worked out] through faith in him, love of him, and through his passion and resurrection. I shall certainly do this, if the lord reveals to me that each and every one of you gather together in common with grace from the name, with one faith, and in Jesus Christ, who is of David's family according to the flesh, son of man and son of God, so that you, with minds at peace, may obey the bishop and the elders, breaking one bread, which is the medicine of immortality, the remedy that prevents death, but gives life forever in Jesus Christ. (20)

19. Farewell in God the father and in Jesus Christ who is our common hope. (21)

To the Magnesians [8]

20. I have learned of your perfectly ordered love of God, and so I have decided, with great joy, to address you. For I have been found deserving of a name most worthy of God, and I sing, in the chains I wear, the praises of the churches; I pray that in them there will exist a union of the flesh and spirit of Jesus Christ, our eternal life, a union of faith and love, which is preferred above all else, and, most important, a union of Jesus and the Father. We shall reach God, if, through him, we withstand the attacks of the prince of this world and make our escape. (1)

[8]Text: *The Apostolic Fathers,* Loeb, I, 196-210.

21. I urge you to do everything eagerly in harmony with God, with the bishop presiding in God's place, with the presbyters in place of the council of the apostles, and with the deacons, who are very dear to me and are entrusted with the service of Jesus Christ, who was with the Father before time and who has appeared at the end. All of you, therefore, should conform yourselves to God's ways and respect one another. Do not look at your neighbor according to the flesh, but love one another always through Jesus Christ. Let nothing exist among you that can divide you; be united with the bishop and with those who preside as models and lessons of immortality. (6)

22. Just as the lord, therefore, was united with the Father and did nothing without him (see Jn. 8.28), either on his own or through the apostles, so you are to do nothing without the bishop and the presbyters. Do not attempt as individuals to show that something is right; let there be in common one prayer, one petition, one mind, one hope in love and in the blameless joy which is Jesus Christ, who surpasses all else. Rush together, all of you, as to one temple of God, to one altar, to one Jesus Christ, who came forth from, is with, and went back to one Father. (7)

23. Do not be deceived by erroneous teachings or by stories which are of no value, for, if we are still living according to the Jewish observance, then we are stating that we did not receive grace. For the holy prophets lived according to Christ Jesus, and they were persecuted for this, because they were inspired by his grace, so that unbelievers might be convinced that there is one God, who revealed himself through Jesus Christ his Son, who is his Word proceeding in silence, and who in every way truly pleased the one who sent him. (8)

24. The people who once lived according to an old order have now attained a new hope; they no longer keep the sabbath, but live for the lord's day, on which our life arose through him and his death, even though some people deny him. Through this mystery we have received faith, and that is why we stand firm, in order to be found as disciples of

Jesus Christ our only teacher. How, then, can we possibly live without him? Even the prophets were his disciples in the spirit and awaited him as a teacher. And this is why he whom the prophets awaited in righteousness raised them from the dead when he came. (9)

25. Let us not fail, therefore, to see his goodness. For, if he ever acted as we do, we would die. Let us, then, become his disciples and learn how to live as Christians; for a person known by any other name than this does not belong to God. Put away the evil leaven, which is old and has turned sour, and change over to the new leaven, which is Jesus Christ (see I Cor. 5.7). Be salted through him, lest any of you be spoiled, since you will be judged according to your savor (see Mt. 5.13). It is wicked to speak of Jesus Christ and to practice Judaism. For Christian faith was not based on Judaism, but Judaism was founded on Christianity; and every tongue that believed in it was gathered to God (see Is. 66.18). (10)

26. Work hard, then, to be strengthened in the teachings of the lord and of the apostles, so that, "in everything you do, you may prosper" (see Ps. 1.3) in flesh and in spirit, in faith and in love, in Son, in Father, and in Spirit, in beginning and in end, along with your most revered bishop, with your elders, the worthily woven spiritual crown, and with the deacons, who belong to God. Obey the bishop and each other, just as Jesus Christ obeyed the Father and as the apostles obeyed Christ and the Father, in order to produce a union of both flesh and spirit. (13)

3. THE LETTER OF BARNABAS[9]

1. The lord put up with the handing over of his flesh to destruction so that we could be cleansed by the forgiveness of sins, that is, through the sprinkling of his blood. A scripture passage about him referred partly to Israel and partly to us; it says, "He was wounded for our trangressions and made

---

[9]Text: *The Apostolic Fathers,* Loeb, I, 354-356. The entire selection is from section 5.

weak because of our sins; we have been healed by his bruises. He was led as a sheep to slaughter, as a dumb lamb before its shearer" (Is. 53.5 and 7). We should be very grateful to the lord, therefore, because he revealed the past to us, made us wise in the present, and did not leave us ignorant with respect to the future.

2. Scripture says, "Not unjustly are nets spread out for birds" (Prov. 1.17). It says this, for people will perish with justice, if they know the way of righteousness, but confine themselves to the way of darkness. Another point, my brethren: the lord put up with suffering for our lives, although he is lord of the universe, to whom God said at the foundation of the world, "Let us make humans according to our image and likeness" (Gen. 1.26). How, then, could he allow himself to suffer at human hands? Here is the answer: the prophets received grace from him and prophesied about him; but in order to destroy death and reveal the resurrection from the dead (see II Tim. 1.10), he allowed what we have described, because he had to appear in flesh (see I Tim. 3.16), in order to fulfill the promise made to the fathers, to prepare for himself a new people, and to show, while on earth, that he will cause the resurrection and will then sit in judgement.

3. Furthermore, he taught Israel and performed such great wonders and signs; he loved Israel very much. But when he chose as his own apostles, who were to preach his gospel, men who were quite lawless and sinful, in order to show that "he did not come to call just people, but sinners" (Mk. 2.17), then he revealed himself to be Son of God. For if he had not come in flesh, how could people have been saved by looking at him, when they cannot look straight into the sun's rays while gazing at it, even though it will cease to exist and is a work of God's hands?

4. The Son of God came in flesh, then, to sum up in their fullness the sins of those who persecuted his prophets through death. That is why he endured what he did. For God says that his flesh was wounded by them: "When they strike their shepherd, then the sheep of the flock will perish"

(see Zech. 13.7). He was willing to suffer in this way, since it was necessary that he suffer on a tree; for the prophet says about him: "Spare my life from the sword" (Ps. 22.20 [LXX, 21.21]), and "Nail my flesh, for congregations of sinners have risen up against me" (see Ps. 119.120 [LXX, 118.120] and Ps. 22.16 [LXX, 21.17]). And again he says, "Behold I have placed my back for scourges and my cheeks for strokes; I have set my face as hard rock" (Is. 50.6-7).

4.THE SO CALLED SECOND LETTER OF CLEMENT OF ROME TO THE CORINTHIANS

1. We must think about Jesus Christ, in the same way that we think about God and about the judge of the living and the dead, and we must not consider our salvation of little value. For if we think him to be of little value, then what we hope to obtain is also of little value. Those who listen as though to unimportant things commit sin, and so do we, when we do not understand from what, by whom, and to what place we have been called, or the sufferings which Jesus endured for us. What return, then shall we pay to him? What fruit shall we offer worthy of what he did for us? What holiness we owe to him! He has graciously given us the light; like a father, he has called us children, and he saved us when we were dying. Through him we know the father of truth. (1.1-4 and 3.1)[10]

2. If Christ, the lord who saved us, was spirit at first, but then became flesh and called us in that way, then we too shall receive our reward in this flesh. (9.5)[11]

3. And so, if we do the will of God our father, we shall be part of the first, spiritual church, created before the sun and the moon. But if we do not do the lord's will, we shall come under the scripture which says, "My house became a den of thieves" (see Mt. 21.13). Let us, then, choose to be part of the church of life, in order to be saved. I am sure that you know

[10]Text: *The Apostolic Fathers,* Loeb, I, 128-132.
[11]Text: *The Apostolic Fathers,* Loeb, I, 142.

that the living church is the body of Christ (see Eph. 1.22-23), for the scripture says, "God made the human being male and female" (Gen. 1.27). The male is Christ, and the female is the church. Furthermore, the books and the apostles say that the church is not a thing of the present, but existed from the beginning. For it was spiritual, as was our Jesus, who appeared in the last days, to save us (see I Pt. 1.20); the church, which is spiritual, appeared in the flesh of Christ, to show us that, if we guard the church in the flesh and keep it free from corruption, we shall receive it back in the holy Spirit. For this flesh is a copy of the Spirit, and, therefore, no one who has corrupted the copy, will receive the original. What he means to say is, "Protect the flesh, in order to share in the Spirit." If we say that the flesh is the church and the Spirit is Christ, then anyone who insults the flesh insults the church. such a person will not, threfore, share in the Spirit, which is Christ. (14.1-4)[12]

5. THE SHEPHERD OF HERMAS

1. The lord has sworn by his Son that those who denied their Christ have been rejected from their life; this refers to those who are now going to deny [the Christ] in the days to come. But, because of his great mercy, [the lord] has been gracious to those who denied [him] in the past. (Vision 2.2.8)[13]

2. [He said], "A man had a field and many servants, and he planted a vineyard in part of the field. He picked out one trustworthy, respected, and honorable servant, summoned him, and said to him, 'Take this vineyard which I have planted, and fence it in, until I return, but do nothing else to it. Keep this command of mine, and I shall set you free.' The servant's master went away to a foreign country, and, after he had gone away, the servant took the vineyard and fenced it in. When he had finished fencing in the vineyard, he saw

---

[12]Text: *The Apostolic Fathers,* Loeb, I, 150-152.

[13]Text: *The Apostolic Fathers,* Loeb, II, 20-22.

that it was full of weeds; so he thought the matter over and said to himself, 'I have fulfilled the master's command; but now I shall dig over this vineyard, and it will be cleaner when that has been done. Without weeds it will give more fruit, since it will not be choked by weeds.' So he went and dug over the vineyard and tore out all the weeds that were in it. And that vineyard was very clean and thriving, since it had no weeds to choke it.

"Sometime later the master of the servant and of the field returned and came to the vineyard. When he saw that the vineyard had been neatly fenced in and had also been dug over, that all the weeds had been torn out, and that the vines were flourishing, he was very pleased with the servant's work. So he summoned his beloved son, who was his heir, and his friends, who were his advisors, and told them what he had commanded his servant and what he found had been done. They too were happy with the servant because of the testimony which the master had given about him. He said to them, 'I promised freedom to this servant, if he obeyed the command which I had given him; he obeyed my command, and, in addition, did excellent work on the vineyard, and has pleased me very much. In return for this work which he did, therefore, I wish to make him a joint heir with my son, for he did not disregard the good idea he had, but brought it to reality.' The master's son agreed with him in his wish that the servant should become a joint heir with the son." (Parable V.2.2-8)[14]

3. [To explain the parable of the vineyard he said], "The field is this world (see Mt. 13.38), and the lord of the field is the one who made all things (see Eph. 3.9), put them in final form, and gave them strength. The son is the holy Spirit.[15] The servant is the Son of God, and the vines are this people whom the Son planted. The fences are the holy angels of the lord, who support the people, and the weeds, which were

[14]Text: *The Apostolic Fathers,* Loeb, II, 154-156.

[15]This sentence is added in one manuscript; without it the identity of the son in the parable remains unexplained. It is in harmony with the next quotation, where the Son seems to be identified with the Spirit.

torn out of the vineyard, are the transgressions of God's servants; the food which he sent him from the banquet represents the commandments which he gave to his people through his Son. The friends and advisors are the holy angels who were created first of all, and the master's journey is the time remaining until his appearance."

"Why, sir," I said, "is the Son of God presented in the parable in the form of a slave" (see Phil. 2.7)?

"Listen," he said; "the Son of God is not presented in the form of a slave, but rather with great power and dominion."

I said, "What do you mean, sir? I do not understand."

"God," he said, "planted the vineyard; in other words, God created the people and gave them to his Son; and the Son set up the angels over them to guard them. He purified their sins by doing hard work and undergoing much suffering, for one cannot dig vineyards without toil and grief. And so, after cleansing the sins of the people, he showed them the paths of life (see Ps. 16.11) and gave them the law, which he had received from his father. You see," he said, "that he is lord of the people himself, since he has received all power from his father (see Jn. 10.18).[16] Hear now the explanation of why the lord took his son and the glorious angels into counsel concerning the inheritance of the servant. God made the preexisting holy Spirit, who created all creation, dwell in the flesh which God chose. This flesh, therfore, in which the holy Spirit resided, served the spirit well, advancing in holiness and purity, and defiling the Spirit in no way. [God], therefore, chose as a partner of the holy Spirit the flesh which had lived well and with purity, which cooperated and worked in harmony with the Spirit in all things, and which behaved with courage and strength; for the conduct of this flesh pleased [God], since it was not defiled even while possessing the holy Spirit on the earth. [God], therefore, took the son and the glorious angels into counsel, so that this flesh, which had served the Spirit blamelessly, might have some place to dwell and might not appear to have lost the reward

---

[16]This sentence is written, correctly it seems, in only one manuscript.

for its service. For all flesh, in which the holy Spirit has dwelt and which is found undefiled and spotless, will receive a reward." (Parable 5.5.2-6.7)[17]

4. After I had written the commandments and the parables of the shepherd who was the angel of repentance, he came to me and told me, "I want to show you what the holy Spirit, who spoke to you in the form of the church, revealed to you; for that spirit is the son of God. Since you were rather weak because of the flesh, an angel did not explain it to you. When you had been strengthened by the Spirit, therefore, and had become strong enough, so that you could see an angel, then the building of the tower was revealed to you through the church."

In the middle of the plain he pointed out to me a large white rock which rose up out of the plain. The rock was higher than the mountains and was square, so that it could encompass the whole world. That rock was old and had a door cut out of it, but it seemed to me that this door had been cut out recently. And the gate shone so much more brightly than the sun, that I marvelled at its brilliance. In a circle around the gate stood twelve virgins. I saw six men coming; they were tall, noble, looked alike, and summoned a large crowd of men, who were also tall, handsome, and strong. The six men ordered the others to build a tower on top of the rock. Then, after a short time, I saw a group of men coming along, and in their midst was a man who was so tall, that his height surpassed the tower. This man examined the building so carefully, that he handled each stone himself. (Parable IX. 1.1-2, 2.1-3, 3.1, 6.1 and 3)[18]

5. I said, "Sir, first of all explain this to me: what is the meaning of the rock and the gate?"

"This rock and gate," he said, "are the Son of God."

"Why, lord," I said, "is the rock old, while the gate is new?"

---

[17]Text: *The Apostolic Fathers*, Loeb, II, 164-168.

[18]Text: *The Apostolic Fathers*, Loeb, II, 216, 220, 222, 230, 232.

"Listen," he said, "and understand, you ignorant man. The Son of God was born long before all his creation, so that he could be the Father's counsellor for the creation that was his; that is why he is old" (see Prov. 8.27).

"But why, sir," I said, "is the gate new?"

"Because," he said, "he appeared in the last days of the fullness; that is why the gate is new, so that those who are going to be saved might enter into the kingdom of God through it. Did you see," he said, "that the stones that came in through the gate were for the building of the tower, while those that did not come in through the gate were sent back again to their original place?"

"Yes, sir," I said.

"In the same way," he said, "none will enter the kingdom of God, unless they receive the holy name of his Son. [The crowd who built the tower] are all glorious angels, and the lord is, therefore, protected by them. But the gate is the Son of God, and this is the only way to the lord; in no other way, then, will anyone come to him, except through his Son. Did you see," he said, "the six men, and in their midst the noble, tall man who walked around the tower and rejected the stones from the building?"

"Yes, sir," I said.

"The noble man is the Son of God, and those six are the glorious angels who support him on the right side and on the left; none of these glorious angels," he said, "will come to God without him. Anyone who does not receive his name will not enter the kingdom of God." (Parable IX. 12.1-4, 6-8)[19]

[19]Text: *The Apostolic Fathers,* Loeb, II, 248-250, 250-252.

Chapter 2

Second Century
Defenders of the Faith

I. Introduction

As Christianity broke definitively from its Jewish foundations in the second half of the second century, it spread
throughout the Roman Empire, and became attractive to
members of the more highly educated and cultured class of
contemporary society. When such people chose to profess
this new faith, they soon found that they had to defend their
decision against the criticism of friends and colleagues who
had not been moved to abandon the traditional Roman religion, because, to those who did not believe, it seemed that
the Christians worshipped a god who was actually a mere
human being. Furthermore, this man was Jewish, and the
Romans despised the Jewish people and their religion.
Finally he ended his life in shame, by being crucified as a
traitor along with two thieves. It thus became imperative for
the newly converted follower of Jesus Christ to explain who
this person was, and why he deserved divine honor. On a less
sophisticated level, popular misunderstanding of the Eucharist and of the communal aspects of Christianity led to
charges of gross immorality.

The authors who sought to justify the faith of second century Christians are commonly called "apologists"; perhaps the best known of them is a certain Justin, who was born a pagan in Samaria, studied Greek philosophy, became a Christian, and taught in Rome, where he was put to death for his faith sometime after the year 160. Justin wrote two "Apologies" (or defenses) on behalf of Christianity and the *Dialogue with Trypho,* which is a (probably fictional) account of a debate between Justin and several devout Jews.

Justin's background led him to stress the reasonableness of Christian faith. A major element in his argument is the identification of Jesus the Christ with God's Word (a rendering of the Greek word 'Logos', which can also mean reason); faith in this Word of God united one with supreme reason (or God) and developed the highest elements of the human person. This approach can be described as a "Word-theology", whose scriptural basis is in the prologue of the gospel according to John, where the "Word" is said to have been with God in the beginning and to be itself divine in some way (Jn. 1.1ff.). Justin, perhaps under the influence of Stoicism, developed this approach to God and the savior in a more philosophical way, and the result was one of the first theological discussions of Christ and salvation. As might be expected, Justin stressed the revelatory function of the Word. His approach was, as noted, philosophical, for he most often used reason rather than revelation as his methodological tool; he was, therefore, not always orthodox by later standards of Christian doctrine, but he never lost sight of the (biblically grounded) identification of God's Word with Jesus, nor of the salvation effected by the death and resurrection of the Christ.

Brief quotes from two other apologists contemporary with Justin will show the importance of Christ and his work to the Christian writers of this period, as well as the lack of clarity which was still characteristic of this area of Christian thought. Athenagoras was a private individual who became a Christian and addressed a plea on behalf of Christianity to the emperors Marcus Aurelius and Lucius Aurelius Commodus. His approach, like Justin's, was philosophical, and the saving work of Jesus the Christ was subordinated to a discussion of the Word, as a basis for proving the reasonableness of Christianity. Athenagoras composed another work on the resurrection of the body, in which Jesus the Christ and his resurrection are not even mentioned. Although he does quote sacred scripture, then, it would appear that the desire to adapt his thought and language to his pagan audience has rendered his Christianity all but invisible. Finally we shall cite Theophilus, bishop of Antioch in Syria. Far from being a philosopher like his contemporaries, Theophilus was apparently influenced primarily by the Old Testament, for, in explaining Christianity to a man named Autolycus, he seems to identify the Word of God with God's Wisdom. The existence of the Word was important for Theophilus, but its true significance was still unclear.

Irenaeus, bishop of Lyons, was a contemporary of Justin, who spoke in a totally different vein, and to another type of audience. He wrote about God's Word, but formed the concept, as he did his entire picture of Christ, from biblical, non-philosophical elements. He developed his view of Christianity in opposition, not to non-Christians, but to gnostic Christians, as they were called, whom he viewed as utterly unorthodox or heretical. Salvation, according to gnostic theory as interpreted by Irenaeus, depended on the acquisition of a special type of knowledge, which could be learned only from one's gnostic teacher. Faith, in this approach, was meaningless, as were the saving acts of Jesus Christ, who, if he figured at all in a particular gnostic system, was usually considered to be a heavenly, non-material being, who posessed the kind of phantom humanity mentioned earlier. Whether or not Irenaeus understood gnosticism and evaluated it correctly, his attitude toward it is clear, and this is one case in the early church where pluralism was not acceptable. For Irenaeus gnosticism was the negation of true Christianity, and the nature and function of Jesus the Christ are dominating factors in the formulation of this judgement.

Salvation was, therefore, a major theme in Irenaeus's writings, as was the Christ who brought it about for those who believe in him. Union with God was still the ultimate goal of life, but the God of Irenaeus was not the gnostic silent abyss, which was beyond all things and was absolutely unapproachable; Irenaeus taught the biblical God, who acted in the Old Testament as creator and lord, and was revealed in the New Testament by the Christ, God's Son, the Word of God made flesh. Faith in this Christ, who died and rose from the dead for all people, was the means whereby union with God was achieved; for Christ, in a famous term employed by Irenaeus, recapitulated, or summed up in himself, all of humanity, with the result that whatever happened to him also touched all those who were joined to him through faith. This view of the importance of Jesus Christ and his work gave Irenaeus an importance in the history of Christian thought which remained unchallenged until recent times, when his condemnation of gnosticism has been interpreted as a product more of partisan politics than of simple dedication to the truth. His major work, from which all the quotes here are taken, is entitled *Against Heresies*. A long quotation about the contents of Luke's gospel is included, to show that concern for the poor and the sinner is intimately connected, for Irenaeus, with saving faith in Christ.

All the authors mentioned thus far wrote in Greek; but there was, of course, a church in the West as well, although the use of Latin in formal and learned discourse was not widespread before the year 200, and its theological center was Carthage in northern Africa rather than Rome. The faith of these Christians grew out of their own experience and understanding of the Christ and his work, and its expression was, therefore, somewhat different from that of their Greek-speaking contemporaries. Not necessarily typical, but extremely influential nonetheless, was the thought of Tertullian, who flourished in Carthage at the end of the second and the beginning of the third century. He does not always represent the faith of the ordinary western Christian, but the concepts he developed and the words he used to express them became all but normative in the West. As orthodox an author as Cyprian of Carthage in the mid-third century viewed Tertullian as his master, and Leo, bishop of Rome at a most crucial time in the history of Christian theology of Christ, i.e., the mid-fifth century, spoke in language which was largely an echo of Tertullian.[1] His influence is all the more striking because of the fact that in his later life he broke from the mainstream, orthodox church of his day and joined a group which was considered heretical; pluralism was not confined to the eastern church. The long quotation here is from the *Apologeticus*, a writing addressed to Roman magistrates in defense of Christianity as a religion.

II. The Writings

1. JUSTIN

First Apology[2]

1. We are called atheists, and we admit that we are atheists when it is a question of gods such as these [i.e., the gods of pagan Rome]. But we are not atheists when it comes to the true God, the father of righteousness, moderation, and the other virtues—the God who is free of all evil. We reverence and worship this God, the Son who came from him and gave us this teaching, the army of other messengers who follow him and are made good like him, and the prophetic Spirit. (6)

2. The Word, who we know to be the most royal and just ruler after the God who begot the Word, proclaims that you will not have success [in overcoming the Christians]. That all this would happen was foretold, I say, by our teacher, the Son and apostle of the lord God, the Father of all, Jesus Christ, after whom we have been named Christians. (12)

---

[1]See the final chapter for further comments about Leo.

[2]Text of both apologies: *The Apologies of Justin Martyr*, ed. B.L. Gildersleeve (1877), *passim*.

3. The one who taught us [faith in God] is Jesus Christ, who was born for this purpose and was crucified under Pontius Pilate, procurator of Judea in the time of Tiberius Caesar. We shall prove that we honor him in a rational way, for we have learned that he is Son of the one who is the true God, and we place him on the second level, with the prophetic Spirit in the third rank. For here is where they say our madness lies, claiming that we give second place after the unchangeable and eternally existing God, who begets all things, to a crucified man; they do not understand the mystery in this. (13)

4. We say that the Word, that is, the firstborn of God, was begotten without sexual intercourse, and that he, Jesus Christ our teacher, was crucified, died, rose, and returned to heaven; in doing this we are not introducing something new like those whom you call sons of Zeus. (21)

5. The Son of God, who is named Jesus, deserves to be called Son of God because of his wisdom, even if he is commonly considered to be only human. For all writers call God the father of human beings and of gods. (22)

6. Jesus Christ is the only true and proper Son born to God, for he is God's Word, firstborn, and power; he became human by his own will in order to convert and restore the human race. (23)

7. We found that in the books of the prophets it was foretold that one was to come, who would be born of a virgin and become a human being; he would heal every disease and sickness, and would raise the dead. He would be hated, go unrecognized, and be crucified—Jesus our Christ—he would die, rise, go up to heaven, and would be and be called the Son of God. It was also foretold that he would send certain people to preach this to the whole human race. (31)

8. What is called a "robe" by the divine Spirit through the prophets (see Genesis 49.11) refers to the people who believe in him; in them dwells the Word, the seed that comes from God. What is called "blood of the grape" is a sign that the one who will appear will have blood, but from divine power,

not from human seed. The first power after the Father of all, the lord God, is a Son, the Word, who took flesh and became human, in a way that we shall explain in what follows. For just as it was not a human being, who made the blood of the vine, but God, so did this intimate that the blood would come, not from human seed, but, as we already said, from God's power. He was conceived, through God's power, by a virgin of the seed of Jacob, the father of Judah, who was shown to be father of the Jews. (32)

9. Some people, who argue without reason for the overthrow of our teachings, could say that we maintain that Christ was born 150 years ago under Cyrenius and that he taught what we claim he taught later on, under Pontius Pilate; they might, therefore, object that, according to us, all those who lived before that time were not held accountable for anything. To keep them from doing this, let us anticipate the problem and solve it. We have been taught and we have proclaimed that the Christ is the firstborn of God and is Word, in which the whole human race participates. Those who lived in accordance with reason are Christians, even if they were considered to be atheists.[3] Examples of such people among the Greeks were Socrates, Heraclitus, and others like them; among non-Greeks, there were Abraham, Ananias, Azarias, Misael, Elias, and many others, whose actions and names we now decline to catalogue, because we know it would take too long.

The ancients who did not live according to reason and killed those who did were, therefore, evil and enemies of Christ; but those who lived according to reason were Christians even in their own time, and lived tranquil lives, free of fear. The intelligent person will be able to understand, from all that has been said here, why, through the power of the Word and in accordance with the will of the lord God, the Father of all, he was born through the virgin as a human being, was named Jesus, was crucified, died, rose, and went up to heaven. (46)

[3]There is a play here on the Greek word *logos*, which can mean "reason", "thought", and "idea," as well as "word".

10. In the name of the lord God, the Father of all, and of our savior Jesus Christ, and of the holy Spirit, they are then washed with the water. This washing is called enlightenment, because the understanding of those who learn these things is enlightened. The enlightened person is washed in the name of Jesus Christ, who was crucified under Pontius Pilate, and in the name of the holy Spirit, who spoke all the prophecies about Jesus through the prophets. (61)

11. God's Word is God's Son, as we have already said; he is also called angel and apostle, since he proclaims whatever must be known, and is sent to reveal what is proclaimed. (63)

12. We call this food eucharist, and only those may share in it who believe that our teachings are true, who have been washed with the bath for forgiveness of sins and rebirth, and who live as the Christ taught. For we do not consider this to be ordinary bread or ordinary drink; just as Jesus Christ our savior became flesh through God's Word and had flesh and blood for our salvation, so we have been taught that the food which was consecrated by the prayer of his word, through which our flesh and blood are changed and nourished, is the flesh and blood of that Jesus who was made flesh. (66)

Second Apology

13. Father, God, creator, lord, and master are not true names, but rather designations derived from good works and actions. His Son, the only one properly called Son, the Word who coexisted and was begotten before creatures, when, in the beginning, he made and formed everything through him (see Prov. 8.22-27), is called Christ, because God anointed him and put all things in order through him; this name also has an unknown meaning, just as the title God is not a name, but rather a human idea implanted in nature, that expresses something difficult to explain. But Jesus, his name as a human and savior, also has meaning. For, as we said earlier, he became human, when he was begotten, in accordance with the will of the one who is God

and Father, on behalf of people who believe, and for the destruction of demons. (6)

14. Our teaching, then, appears to be greater than all human teaching, because Christ, who appeared for us, became the whole rational being, body, reason, and soul. For anything that philosophers and lawgivers have ever discovered or expressed well, was elaborated by them through some contact with reason in their discovery and vision.[4] But since they did not recognize reason in the totality, which is Christ, they often contradicted themselves. Those who lived before Christ, and who tried in a human way, through reason, to discover and test the truth, were brought into court as irreverent meddlers. Socrates, who was the most industrious of all people in this endeavor, was accused of the same things as we are. (10)

15. I admit that I boast and fight with all my strength to be found a Christian, not because Plato's teachings are different from Christ's, but because they are not similar in every way, which is also true of the others, such as the Stoics, poets, and historians. For each one spoke well in accordance with his share of the seed of divine reason and what he saw was related to it; but those who contradicted themselves in more important matters do not appear to have possessed reliable wisdom and irrefutable knowledge. Whatever people have said well belongs to us Christians, since after God we worship and love the Word who is from the unbegotten and ineffable God; for the Word became human on our behalf, in order to share in our sufferings and provide a cure for them. All the writers could see reality indistinctly through the sowing of the implanted reason that was in them. For the seed of something and its imitation, given according to capacity, are one thing; but the reality, in which there are participation and imitation according to the grace which comes from that reason, is another thing altogether. (13)

[4]See note 3 above.

Dialogue with Trypho

16. I am proving from all the scriptures, that Christ was preached as ruler, priest, God, lord, angel, human, captain, and stone; he was preached as a child who was born and who became, first of all, subject to suffering; he then goes back up to heaven, and comes again with glory and with eternal dominion. He has rescued the beggar from the powerful, and has saved the poor man who has no one to help him. He will spare the beggar and the poor, and will save the lives of the poor. He will redeem their lives from usury and injustice, and his name will be honored before them. (34)[5]

17. Those who acted in a way that was universally, naturally, and eternally good are pleasing to God and will be saved through this Christ in the resurrection, in the same way as the righteous people of the past, such as Noah, Enoch, Jacob, and others like them, along with those who have come to recognize this Christ as God's Son, who existed before the morning-star (see Ps. 109.3 [LXX]) and the moon, and who submitted to becoming flesh and to being born through this virgin of David's family, so that through this plan the serpent which sinned in the beginning, and the angels like it, might be destroyed, and that death might be despised. (45)[6]

18. Trypho said, "We have heard what you think about this, but now, take up the discussion where you left off and finish it. For it seems to me that it is self-contradictory and absolutely impossible to prove. Your claim that this Christ is God and exists before the ages, and that he then submitted to being born and became human, and that he is not a human from a human seems to me to be not only self-contradictory, but stupid as well."

I replied to this, "I know that these statements seem self-contradictory, especially to your people. Now, Trypho," I said, "there is no doubt that this man is God's Christ, even if I cannot prove absolutely that he, as God, was preexistent

[5]Text: PG, 6.548.
[6]Text: PG, 6.572-573.

Son of the creator of the universe and became human through the virgin. In light, however, of all that has been proved, namely, that he is the Christ of God, whoever he is, even if I do not prove that he preexisted and that he submitted, according to the Father's will, to being born with flesh, a human person subject to suffering, as we are, it is right to say that I was wrong only in this, but not to deny that he is the Christ, even if he appears as a human being born of human parents, and is proved to have become Christ through selection. For," I said, "even some of our own people, my friends, confess that he is Christ, while declaring that he was a human being from human parents; but I do not agree with them, and most of those who think as I do would not say this either, since we were commanded by Christ himself to believe, not human teachings, but those proclaimed by the holy prophets and taught by himself." (48)[7]

19. "My friends," I said, "I shall give you another testimony from the scriptures, to the effect that, before all things, God begot a beginning, a type of rational power from himself, which the holy Spirit calls glory of the lord, Son, wisdom, angel, God, lord, and Word. For he can be called by all these titles, since he serves the Father's wishes and was begotten by the Father's will. We see the same thing happening with us; for when we bring forth an idea, we beget a word, but not in the form of an excision, as though we were made smaller by bringing forth the word that is in us. My witness for this is the Word of wisdom, which is itself this God born of the Father of all, and is also Word, wisdom, power, and glory of the begetter. (61)[8]

[7]Text: PG, 6.580-581.
[8]Text: PG, 6.613-616.

2. ATHENAGORAS

A Plea on behalf of Christians[9]

1. We have given enough proof that we are not atheists by presenting one God, unbegotten, eternal, invisible, not subject to change, incomprehensible, and infinite; this God is grasped only by mind and reason, and is clothed in light, beauty, and indescribable power. All things were made and ordered, and are ruled by him through the Word which is his. But we think that there is also a Son of God, and no one should think that the idea of God's having a Son is foolish. Our views of either God the Father or the Son are not produced as are the myths composed by the poets, who portray the gods as no better than humans. No, the Son of God is the Father's Word in form and activity, for all things were made by him and through him (see Jn. 1.3), since the Father and Son are one (see Jn. 10.30).

And since the Son is in the Father and the Father in the Son (see Jn. 10.38) through unity and the power of the Spirit, the Son of God is the Father's mind or Word. But if, in your infinite wisdom, you decide to study what "Son" means, I shall tell you briefly: the Son is the first begotten of the Father. This does not mean that the Son came into existence, for God, as eternal mind, from the very beginning possessed the Word internally, since God was eternally rational; instead the Son came forth to be form and activity for all material things. The prophetic Spirit agrees with this account, for it says, "The lord made me in the beginning of his ways for his works" (Prov. 8.22). And we say that this holy Spirit, which works in those who prophesy, is and flows out of God, pouring forth and returning back like a ray of the sun. Who, then, would not be astonished to hear the name of atheist applied to people who introduce a God the Father, a God the Son, and a God the holy Spirit, and who teach that they are united in power, but different in rank. (10.1-5)

[9]Text: OECT, 20-22, 58.

2. We say that there is a God, and a Son, God's Word, and a holy Spirit, who we say are united in power, but distinguished by rank into the Father, the Son, and the Spirit, since the Son is mind, Word, and wisdom of the Father, while the Spirit is an emanation, like light from a fire. (24.2)

3. THEOPHILUS

To Autolycus[10]

1. God had his immanent Word within his own bowels and begot it along with his wisdom, uttering it before all things (see Ps. 45.2 [LXX, 44.2]). God used this Word to assist in what God made, and through it God made all things (see Jn. 1.3). This Word is called beginning, because it begins and rules over all things made through it. This Word, therefore, was Spirit of God, beginning (see Col. 1.18), wisdom, and power of the most high (see I Cor. 1.24), and it came down into the prophets and spoke through them about the creation of the world and about everything else. For the prophets did not exist when the world came into being; what did exist were God's wisdom which is in God, and God's holy Word which is always with God (see Prov. 8.27 and Jn. 1.1-2). (II.10)

2. God's Word, through whom God made all things (see Jn. 1.3), is God's power and wisdom (see I Cor. 1.24); this Word, then, assumed the character of the Father and lord of all, was present in the garden in God's character, and conversed with Adam. For divine scripture itself teaches us that Adam said he heard the voice (see Gen. 3.10). And what else is the voice but the Word of God, which is also God's Son? This is to be understood, not as the poets and writers of myth, who speak of sons of gods born through sexual intercourse, but rather as truth describes the Word, which is immanent power in God's heart. For before anything came

[10]Text: OECT, 38-40, 62-64.

Second Century Defenders of the Faith 55

into being, God had this as a counsellor (see Wis. 8.9), since it was God's mind and intelligence.

Whenever God wished to make what God had decided to make, God begot the Word and brought it forth into being, firstborn of all creation (see Col. 1.15); God did not get rid of the Word, but rather begot God's Word and converses with it forever. We are taught, therefore, by holy scripture and by inspired people, as one of them, John, says, "In the beginning was the Word, and the Word was with God" (Jn. 1.1); he shows that at the start God was alone and the Word was in God. Then he says, "And the Word was God; all things were made through it, and without it was made nothing" (Jn. 1.3). Since the Word, therefore, is God and born from God, whenever the Father of all wills to do so, he sends the Word to some place, and the Word is present and is heard and seen there, for it is sent by God and is situated in a place. (II.22)

4. IRENAEUS OF LYONS

Against Heresies

1. John proclaims one almighty God and one only begotten, Christ Jesus, through whom he says all things were made (see Jn. 1.3); and he says that this latter one is the Word of God, the only begotten, the maker of all, the true light which enlightens every human being, the one who fashioned the world, the one who came to his own, the one who became flesh and dwelt among us (see Jn. 1.1-14). But the Gnostics pervert this with specious explanations and claim that, through emission, there is another only begotten one, whom they call Beginning; they also claim that there is another Savior, another Logos or Word, Son of the only begotten, and another Christ, emitted to perfect the Pleroma. And so they snatched away from the truth each one of the statements just cited, misused the titles, and adapted them to their own interpretation; according to them, therefore, although John spoke so much about this, he never

mentioned the lord Jesus Christ. For when he spoke of Father, grace, only begotten, truth, Word, life, human, and church, he was talking, according to their interpretation, about the first Ogdoad,[11] in which there was not yet a Jesus, or a Christ, the teacher of John.

But the apostle himself made it quite clear that he was not talking about the gnostic groupings, but about our lord Jesus Christ, who he knew was also the Word of God. For he came back to the Word which he said had existed in the beginning and commented, "And the word became flesh and dwelt among us" (Jn. 1.14). According to their interpretation, however, the Word did not become flesh, because it never even came outside the Pleroma; what became flesh [according to them] was the Savior who was made out of all those in the Pleroma and who existed later than the Word. (I.9.2)[12]

2. Learn then, you foolish people, that Jesus, who suffered for us and who dwelt among us, was himself the Word of God. For if some other one from among the Aeons had become flesh for our salvation, then one would have had to think that the apostle spoke of someone else. But if the Word of God who came down is the same one who goes up (see Jn. 3.13), the only-begotten Son of the one God, made flesh for human beings according to the Father's good will, then John was not speaking about someone else or about the Ogdoad, but about the lord Jesus Christ. According to them, furthermore, the Word did not become flesh in a proper sense, for they say that the savior put on an animal body, formed according to a plan by some ineffable providence, in order to become visible and tangible. But flesh is that ancient creation, made by God from soil in Adam (see Gen. 2.7), and John proclaimed that the Word of God truly became this. And so their primal and elemental Ogdoad is destroyed. For, since Word, only-begotten, life, light, savior, and Christ the Son of God are shown to be one and the

[11]The Ogdoad was a gnostic grouping of primary heavenly beings.

[12]Text: SC, 264, 138-143.

same, and since this same person became flesh for us, the fabrication that is their Ogdoad is destroyed. (I.9.3)[13]

3. There is one and the same God, the Father of our lord, who promised through the prophets to send a forerunner, and who caused his salvation, that is, his Word, to become visible to all flesh; the Word itself became flesh, so that the king of all things might become known in them. For it was proper that those who are judged see the judge and know by whom they are judged, and that those who are attaining glory should know the one who gives them the gift of glory. (III.9.1)[14]

4. And then, with respect to the baptism, Matthew says, "The heavens were opened, and he saw the Spirit of God as a dove descending and coming upon him. And behold there was a voice from heaven which said, 'You are my Son, the beloved one, in whom I am well pleased'" (Mt. 3.16-17). For the Christ did not descend upon Jesus at that time, nor was the Christ one person and Jesus another; the Word of God, who is savior of all and ruler of heaven and earth, who is Jesus, as we have already showed, and who assumed flesh and was anointed by the Father in the spirit—[this Word] became Jesus Christ. Insofar as the Word of God was a human being from the root of Jesse and a son of Abraham, the Spirit of God rested upon him, and he was anointed to preach the gospel to the lowly (see Lk. 4.18). But inasmuch as he was God, he did not judge according to glory or condemn according to hearsay; for "he did not need anyone to give testimony about human beings, since he knew what was in them" (Jn. 2.25). Instead, he called all people who grieve, and, granting them forgiveness from the sins which brought them into captivity, he freed them from the chains of which Solomon said, "All are restrained by the bonds of their own sins" (see Prov. 5.22). There descended on him, therefore, the Spirit of that God who had promised through the

[13]Text: SC, 264, 142-146.
[14]Text: SC, 211, 102-103.

prophets to anoint him, so that we might receive from his rich anointing and be saved. (III.9.3)[15]

5. Who else can reign in the house of Jacob uninterrupt-edly and forever except Jesus Christ, our lord, Son of the most high God (see Lk 1.32-33), who promised through the law and the prophets to make his own salvation visible to all flesh, so that he would become a son of man in order that the human being might become a son of God? (III.10.2)[16]

6. If one rejects Luke on the pretext that he did not know the truth, then one will certainly reject the gospel whose disciple he claims to be. For through him we have learned many essential elements of the gospel, such as the birth of John, the story of Zachariah, the angel's coming to Mary and Elizabeth's cry, the descent of the angels to the shep-herds and what they said to them, the testimony of Anna and Simeon about Christ, that he was left behind in Jerusa-lem at the age of twelve, the baptism of John, the age at which the lord was baptized, and that it took place in the fifteenth year of Tiberius Caesar. With respect to his teach-ing there are these sayings to the wealthy: "Woe to you, the wealthy, for you see your consolation. Woe to you who have been filled, for you will be hungry, and to you who laugh now, for you will weep. Woe to you when all people bless you; this is the way your ancestors dealt with the false prophets" (Lk. 6.24-26). All things like this we know only through Luke.

We have also learned through him many acts of the lord which all people accept: the multitude of fish which Peter's companions caught when the lord ordered them to let down their net; the woman who had suffered for eighteen years and was cured on the sabbath; the man with dropsy whom the lord cured on the sabbath day, and how he defended his working a cure on that day; how he taught the disciples not to seek the first places; how one should invite the poor and the weak who can make no repayment; the man who knocks at night to obtain bread, and who obtains it because of the insistence with which he asks; that, when he was dining at the Pharisee's house, a sinful woman kissed his feet and anointed them with perfume, and all that he said to Simon because of her on the subject of the two debtors; the parable of that rich man who locked up whatever had come to him, and to whom it was said, "In this night they will demand your life from you; as for the things which you have prepared, to whom will they belong?" (Lk. 12.20); a similar parable of a rich man who is clothed in purple and feasts lavishly, and of the poor man Lazarus; the response which he gave to his disciples when they said to him, "Increase our faith" (Lk. 17.5); the conversation he had with the publican Zacchaeus; the pharisee and the publican who worshipped together in the temple; the ten lepers whom he cleansed at one time on the road; that he ordered the lame and the blind to be brought together from the streets and byways to the marriage feast; the parable about the judge who did not fear God, but who was driven by the widow's persistence to vindicate her; the fig tree in the vineyard which did not bear fruit; many other things which can be found to have been said by Luke alone, but which Marcion and Valentinus also use; in addition to all this, what he said to his disciples after the resurrection on the road, and how they recognized him in the breaking of the bread. (III.14.3)[17]

7. That John knew only one and the same Word of God, the only-begotten who became flesh for our salvation, Jesus Christ our lord, we have proved sufficiently from the words of John himself. But Matthew too recognizes only one and the same Christ Jesus, and portrays his human birth from the virgin, by saying, "The book of the birth of Jesus Christ, son of David, son of Abraham" (Mt. 1.1). (III.16.2)[18]

8. Paul says in the letter to the Galatians, "When the fullness of time came, God sent his Son, born of woman and under the law, to redeem those who were under the law, so

[17]Text: SC, 211, 266-273.
[18]Text: SC, 211, 290-293.

that we might receive adoption" (Gal. 4.4-5). By this he clearly portrays one God who made a promise about his Son through the prophets, and one Jesus Christ our lord, who is descended from David through his birth from Mary and designated Son of God in power, this Jesus Christ, according to the Spirit of holiness, through the resurrection from the dead; and so he is the firstborn of the dead, just as he is also the firstborn in all creation, the Son of God become a son of man, so that through him we might receive adoption, since the human sustains, seizes, and embraces the son of God. (III.16.3)

9. [Heretics] wander far away from the truth, since their opinions deviate from the one who is truly God; they do not know that God's Word, the only begotten, who is always present to the human race, was united and mingled with its own creation in accord with the Father's good pleasure, and became flesh. This Word is itself Jesus Christ our lord, who suffered for us, rose for us, and will come again in the glory of the Father, to revivify all flesh, to declare salvation, and to extend the rule of just judgement over all who were subjected to him. There is, therefore, one God the Father, as we have shown, and one Christ Jesus our lord, who comes through a universal plan and recapitulates all things in himself. But in every way he is also a human, a creation of God; he, therefore, recapitulated humanity in himself. The invisible became visible, the incomprehensible became comprehensible, the unchangeable became subject to change, and the Word became human, recapitulating everything in himself. And so, just as the Word of God is first in the supercelestial, spiritual, and invisible world, so does the Word have primacy in the visible and corporeal world; in taking the primacy on himself and making himself head of the church, he draws everything to himself at the proper time. (III.16.6)[19]

10. As we have said, therefore, he joined and united humanity with God. For if a human being had not con-

[19]Text: SC, 211, 312-315.

quered humanity's enemy, then that enemy would not have been overcome justly; but, at the same time, if God had not bestowed salvation, our possession of it would not have been secure. And if humanity had not been united to God, it could not have achieved a sharing of incorruptibility. For through his relationship with each of them "the mediator between God and human beings" (I Tim. 2.5) had to lead them to both friendship and harmony, presenting humanity to God and revealing God to humans. For how could we share in God's filial adoption, if we had not received from God, through the Son, communion with God, and if God's Word had not become flesh and shared that with us?

He who was going to destroy sin and redeem the humanity that was subject to death had to become that very reality in question, a human being who had been dragged into slavery by sin and held captive by death, so that sin might be destroyed by a human being and humanity might escape from death. For just as many became sinners and lost life through the disobedience of one person who was formed first from the elements of the earth, so it was proper that many be justified and receive salvation through the obedience of one person (see Rom. 5.19), who was the first one born of a virgin. The Word of God became human, in keeping with Moses's words, "God, his works are true" (Dt. 32.4). If he only appeared as though he were flesh, without having become flesh, then his work was not true. But he actually was what he appeared to be, namely, God, recapitulating in himself the model of humanity formed long ago, in order to kill sin, destroy death, and give life to humanity. And for this reason his works are true. (III.18.7)[20]

11. But in the last time, when the fullness of the time of freedom had come, the Word itself, by itself, washed away the filth of the daughters of Zion, washing the feet of its disciples as its own hands. For this is the goal of the human race that has God as its inheritance: just as in the beginning, through the first humans, we were all brought into slavery

[20]Text: SC, 211, 364-371.

by the penalty of death, so at the end, through the last one, all who were his disciples from the beginning are to be washed and cleansed from everything pertaining to death and come to God's life. For he who washed his disciples' feet sanctified the whole body and made it clean (see Jn. 13.3-10). (IV.22.1)[21]

12. For Christ did not come only for those who believed in him in the age of Tiberius Caesar, nor did the Father's providence extend only to people who are now alive; they acted, rather, for all human beings, who, from the beginning, according to their ability and in their own time, feared and loved God, acted justly and decently toward their neighbors, and desired to see Christ and to hear his voice. At the second coming, therefore, he will first of all wake all such people from their sleep, will raise them together with the rest who will be judged, and will establish them in his kingdom. (IV.22.2)[22]

13. For we could not have learned about God in any other way, if our teacher, existing as the Word, had not become a human being, since no one could have told us about the Father except his very own Son. For who else has known the mind of the lord, and who else has become his counsellor? Once again, there was no other way for us to have learned than by seeing our teacher and by hearing his voice with our own ears, so that, by imitating his works and doing what he said, we could thus be united to him; in this way we, who were made only recently, could increase through the perfect one who existed before all creation, and could be formed into his likeness by the one who alone is most good and who has the gift of incorruptibility. This is for us who were indeed predestined to exist according to the Father's foreknowledge, although we did not yet exist, but were made and began to exist in the times known in advance, through the service of the Word.

[21] Text: SC, 100, 684-686.

[22] Text: SC, 100, 688-690.

This Word is perfect, since it is a powerful Word and a true human being; redeeming us through his blood in a way befitting his nature, he gave himself as a redemption for those who were led into captivity. Since defection [from God] ruled over us unjustly and, although we actually belonged to God, had alienated us unnaturally by making us its own disciples, the Word of God, powerful in all things and not deficient in its own justice, turned with justice against that defection, winning back its own belongings from it, not by force (as defection had conquered us in the beginning, greedily seizing what did not belong to it), but by persuasion, as was proper for the God who persuades and does not apply force to attain what he wishes, so that justice should not be thwarted, and that that ancient creation of God should not perish.

The lord, therefore, redeems us by his blood and gives his soul for our souls and his flesh for our flesh; he pours out the Father's Spirit to create unity and communion between God and human beings. He brings God down to humans through the Spirit, and at the same time raises humans toward God by his incarnation; at his coming he truly and surely gives us incorruptibility through communion with him. Because of this the teachings of all heretics are destroyed. (V.1.1)[23]

14. God will be glorified in his creation, shaping it to be the same form as, and similar to his own Son. For through the hands of God, i.e., the Son and the Spirit, a human being, not merely a part of one, is made in God's likeness. A soul and a spirit can be parts of a human being, but can in no way be full human beings; a complete human being is a mixture and a union of the soul, which assumes the Spirit of the Father, and which is mingled with that flesh which is made in God's image. (V.6.1)[24]

15. That the apostle did not proclaim against the very substance of flesh and blood that it does not possess the kingdom of God (see I Cor. 15.50) is proved by the fact that

[23] Text: SC, 153, 16-21.
[24] Text: SC, 153, 72-73.

the same apostle everywhere used the phrase "flesh and blood" to refer to our lord Jesus Christ; he did this, partly to establish his humanity (since he called himself "son of man"), and partly to verify the salvation of our flesh. For if the flesh could not be saved, the Word of God would never have become flesh, and if the blood of the just did not require an accounting, the lord would never have had blood. The lord said to those who were going to shed his blood, "An account will be demanded of all the just blood shed on the earth, from the blood of Abel the just one to the blood of Zechariah, son of Barachiah, whom you killed between the sanctuary and the altar; I say to you, all these things will come on this generation" (see Mt. 23.35 and Lk. 11.50-51). Thus he shows that the blood of all just people and of the prophets shed from the beginning will be summed up in himself, and that an account would be demanded for their blood through himself. This account would not be demanded, if it could not be saved, nor would the lord have recapitulated this in himself, if he had not become flesh and blood like the original creation, thus saving in himself at the end what had perished in Adam at the beginning. (V.14.1)[25]

16. But if the lord became flesh because of some other plan, or if he took flesh from another substance, then he did not recapitulate humanity in himself; in this case, indeed, he could not even be called flesh. For flesh is properly the descendant of the first creation made from the earth. If he had had to take the material from another substance, then the Father in the beginning would have seen to it that his working material was made from another substance. But now the saving Word has become the very thing which had perished, i.e., humanity, and has produced through itself that participation in itself and the discovery of humanity's salvation. That which had perished had flesh and blood, for God took soil from the earth and formed humanity; the whole purpose of the lord's coming is aimed at humanity. And so he himself had flesh and blood, recapitulating in

[25]Text: SC, 153, 182-186.

himself, not some other creation, but that first one, and looking for that which had perished. (V.14.2)[26]

17. For the creator of the world is truly the Word of God, and this is our lord, who in the last time became human and lived in this world; in an unseen way he contains all created things and is stamped into all creation, since God's Word governs and disposes of everything. And so he came to his own (see Jn. 1.11) in an unseen way, became flesh (see Jn. 1.14), and hung upon a cross, in order to recapitulate everything in himself. (V.18.3)[27]

5. TERTULLIAN

Apologeticus[28]

1. Even ordinary people are now aware of Christ as a human being, which is the way the Jews saw him; as a result one might easily conclude that we worship a human. But we are not ashamed of Christ, since we are delighted to be classified under his name and to be condemned because of it; nor is our conception of God different from the Jewish one. A few words about Christ as God are, therefore, required. (xxi.3)

2. God had announced that someone would come to reshape and enlighten human activity, and so this Christ, the Son of God, came. The Son of God was proclaimed in advance as the one who would distribute and teach the grace of this way of life, and enlighten and lead the human race. He was not born in such a way as to arouse shame over the title of son or because of the paternal seed; it was not through incest with a sister, or through the corruption of a daughter or another's wife that he had to endure a divine father clothed with scales, horns, or feathers, a lover who turned into gold for a daughter of Danaus. These are the

[26]Text: SC, 153, 186-188.
[27]Text: SC, 153, 244-245.
[28]Text: *Tertullian. Apologeticus and De Spectaculis,* Loeb, 102-114.

doings of Jupiter and they affect your gods. But the Son of God does not have a mother as a result of impurity; even the mother who appears to be his did not consummate her marriage. (xxi.7-9)

3. Let me speak first about his essence, for in this way the way in which he was born will become more intelligible. We have already stated that God constructed this whole universe by word, reason, and power. Among your wise men, too, it is agreed that *Logos*, that is, word and reason, appears to be the shaper of the universe. For Zeno designates *Logos* as maker, the one who shaped everything in an orderly way, and declares that it is called fate, God, the mind of Jupiter, and universal necessity. Cleanthes brings these elements together in spirit, which, according to him, permeates the universe. (xxi.10)

4. As for us, we also attribute spirit, as its own essential reality, to the word, reason, and power, through which we have asserted God made everything; word is in spirit when it proclaims, reason assists spirit when it makes order, and power directs spirit when it makes perfect. We have learned that this was expressed by God, was begotten by this expression, and is, therefore, Son of God and is called God, because they are united in essence. For God is also spirit. (xxi.11)

5. When a ray streams from the sun, it is a part of the whole; the sun will be in the ray, because it is a ray of the sun and is not cut off from its essence, but is rather an extension of it. Thus spirit is from spirit and God is from God, as light is kindled from light. The source of the matter in question remains complete and inexhaustible, even if you borrow from it many branches of its nature. What has proceeded from God, therefore, is God and Son of God, and the two are one. Spirit has made a second numerical unit from spirit, then, as God has from God, but by a process of ranking, not by a change in constitution; they did not withdraw from the source, they flowed out of it. That ray of God, therefore, descended, as had always been predicted in the past, into a certain virgin, was formed into flesh in her womb, and was

born, a human being mingled with God. Flesh, filled with spirit, is fed, grows up, talks, teaches, acts, and is Christ. (xxi.12-14)

6. Because of his humility the Jewish people had assumed that he was only a human being; it was logical, then, for them to consider him a magician because of his power. For with a word he drove demons out of people, gave sight back to the blind, cured lepers, and strengthened paralytics; with a word he actually restored the dead to life; he tamed the very elements [of nature], curbing the storms and walking on the sea. Thus he showed that he is the Word of God, or the *Logos*, that original, first-begotten being, accompanied by power and reason, and supported by the Spirit, the same one who, with a word, continued to make all things as he had made them. (xxi.17)

7. We worship God through Christ. We say this and we say it openly; torn and bloody we shout it out, even while you are torturing us. Consider Christ a human, if you wish; through him and in him God wishes to be known and worshipped. (xxi. 28)

Chapter 3

The Earliest Christian Theologians

I. Introduction

The writers quoted in this chapter have as their ultimate purpose more than the mere exposition or defense of Christianity, for they seek a deeper understanding of their faith, and use a kind of philosophical analysis to attain it. But, however influenced they may be by the classical schools of Platonic or Stoic thought, they remain Christians, seeking God and salvation through Christ. For this reason they are described here as the earliest Christian theologians.

Melito of Sardis is a shadowy contemporary of Justin and Irenaeus. His homily on the paschal mystery speaks at length of the saving work of Christ, but in language more resonant of the fifth century than of his own. This document is another witness to the diversity which can be found in the early church's expression of the experience it had with the saving person and work of Jesus Christ. The context of the selections here is the contrast between the saving events symbolized by the paschal lamb of the old covenant and the salvation effected by Jesus which, according to the Christians, it foreshadowed.

Around the year 200 there flourished in Alexandria, the cultural capital of Egypt at that time, a Greek philosopher turned Christian, whose name was Clement. His audience was an educated one, and his writings, in which he often attacked the same type of Gnosticism opposed by Irenaeus, reflect his own intellectual formation. He refers to the savior most often as God's Word, or reason, who is the image of God, existed eternally with God, and became human for the sake of human salvation. This Word, clothed in flesh, teaches human beings by revealing God to them and by leading them to God. Clement believed in the true humanity of the Word become flesh, although the influence of Platonism and Stoicism on him sometimes led to ambivalent statements in this regard. For Clement, faith in the Logos become flesh was, in principle, the key to salvation, but he emphasized the Word's teaching and human understanding of that teaching, rather than Jesus Christ's dying and rising from the dead.

Three of Clement's extant writings will be cited here: the *Exhortation to the Heathen,* which maintains that the pagan classics have been replaced by a new source of knowledge, the "new song" of Jesus Christ, the Christian savior; the *Instructor,* which develops the role of Christ as teacher about God; *Who is the rich man who can be saved?,* a short commentary on Christ's words about the possibilities of salvation open to the wealthy.

Clement was an enigmatic figure, for he was a dedicated Christian, whose inspiration often seems to spring more from Greek philosophy than from Christ and the scriptures; he was a champion of orthodox faith, whose thought was largely out of the mainstream which was slowly being formed. He opposed a Gnosticism which he found heretical, but could nonetheless refer to the perfect Christian as a gnostic. He demanded faith, but looked beyond it to knowledge. At this stage of Christian history, then, the Christian experience of Christ and salvation continues to appear as a complex and fluid reality, even when clothed in the philosophical structures developed by a Clement.

The final figure of interest in the period prior to the year 300, and the most important one of all, is Origen, a native of Alexandria and a generation younger than Clement, who became one of the most dominant figures in the history of early Christian thought. He was raised as a Christian, was well educated, and became a scholar of the highest rank. For reasons which cannot be ascertained with absolute certitude today, he fell afoul of Alexandrian church authority and was considered suspect in his own lifetime. In succeeding generations some of his teachings were considered heretical, and, since he was revered by some and condemned by others, many of his writings were either altered or lost, depending on the attitude of those who handled them. But none could ignore him, as is shown by the fact that he was officially condemned by a general council of the church some 300 years after his death.

As indicated above, Origen was a learned and meticulous scholar. He was well read in Greek philosophy, whose influence left a mark on his work; because he was a Christian, however, almost all of his extant work consists of scriptural exegesis, whose ultimate goal was to enable Origen and his reader to achieve mystical union with God through Christ. Like Clement, therefore, Origen used the image of the Logos as mediator between human beings and a God who is completely transcendent.

Since the Logos, as God, surpasses created, human capabilities, the point of contact with the mediator comes through the human soul, which is superior to flesh and can attain the divine realm. At the same time, the reality of human flesh requires some human element in the goal sought; the Word through whom one attains God, therefore, is the incarnate Word, who must possess real human flesh, truly united with the divine reality. This union is possible because Origen believed that every human soul, and the human soul of Jesus, existed prior to the conception and birth of the human person of which it is a part; it could, therefore, in its preexistent state of innocence be totally united to the Word. This explanation of the origin of the human soul and of the unity of the human and divine in the incarnate Word was rejected by Christianity after Origen as nonorthodox. Be that as it may, his vision of Christ and salvation adds still another dimension to the picture that has been emerging here.

All the quotations of Origen are taken from his book *Against Celsus,* a defense of Christianity written in response to the criticisms of a pagan philosopher. Unlike most of Origen's writings, this is not a commentary on scripture; but he does quote the bible frequently, and the apologetic nature of the book provides him with the occasion to clarify his thoughts about the saving actions of God and the Christ, as well as the unities which bestow salvation, and in which salvation consists.

II. The Writings

1. MELITO OF SARDIS

On Passover

1. There was a son instead of a lamb, and a human instead of a sheep; in the human was Christ who has encompassed everything. And so the slaying of the sheep, the displaying of the blood, and the writing of the law have come down to Jesus Christ, through whom all things existed (see Heb. 2.10) in the ancient law, or rather, in the new word. For the law has become word and the old has become new, since they went out together from Zion and Jerusalem (see Is. 2.3 and Mic. 4.2); the commandment has become grace, the image has become reality, the lamb has become a son, the sheep has become a human, and the human being has become God. For he was born as a son, was led as a lamb, was slain as a sheep, was buried as a human being, and rose from the dead as God, being by nature God and a human being. He is all things: as one who judges, he is law; as one who teaches, he is Word; as one who saves, he is grace; as one who begets,

he is father; as one who is begotten, he is son; as one who suffers, he is sheep; as one who is buried, he is a human being; as one who rises, he is God. This is Jesus the Christ, to whom be glory forever and ever. Amen. (5-10)[1]

2. Many prophets made many other announcements about the Passover, which is Christ. To him be glory forever. Amen. He came from heaven to the earth because of the one who was suffering; he clothed himself in that very one through a virgin's womb and came forth a human being; he accepted the passions of the one who was suffering through the body which could suffer, and he destroyed the passions of the flesh; through the Spirit which could not die he killed death, the killer of human beings. (65-66)[2]

3. He is the one who became flesh in a virgin, was hanged on a tree, was buried in the earth, was raised from the dead, and was assumed to the heights of heaven. (70)[3]

4. The one who hung the earth in place is hanging; the one who fixed the heavens has been fixed; the one who made the universe fast has been fastened to a tree; the master has been insulted; God has been murdered. (96)[4]

2. CLEMENT OF ALEXANDRIA

Exhortation to the Heathen

1. The Word of God, the descendant of David, who also existed before David, scorned the lyre and the harp (instruments without souls) and brought into harmony through a holy Spirit this world of ours, and especially the microcosm of the human being, composed of a body and a soul. The Word sings hymns to God on this multi-toned instrument, and sings together with the instrument that is the human being. The lord gave the breath of life to the human being

[1] Text: OECT, 4-6.
[2] Text: OECT, 34.
[3] Text: OECT, 36-38.
[4] Text: OECT, 54.

and made it, a beautiful instrument, according to his own image (see Gen. 1.17 and 2.7). He himself is surely God's harmonious instrument, in tune and holy, transcendent wisdom, heavenly Word. (1.5.3-4)[5]

2. What then does the instrument, God's Word, the lord and new song, desire? To open the eyes of the blind and to unplug the ears of the deaf; to lead the lame or those who wander to righteousness; to show God to foolish human beings; to stop corruption and to conquer death; to reconcile disobedient sons to a father. God's instrument loves human beings. The lord shows pity, teaches, exhorts, admonishes, saves, protects, and from abundance promises us the kingdom of heaven as a reward for our learning; in return the lord receives from us only one thing—our salvation. For evil feeds on the destruction of human beings, while truth, like the bee that harms nothing, delights only in the salvation of human beings. You have the promise, therefore, and the love for humanity; share in the good favor. And do not imagine that my saving song is something new, like furniture or a house, for it existed "before the morning-star" (Ps. 110.3 [LXX, 109.3]), and "in the beginning was the Word, and the Word was with God, and the Word was God" (Jn. 1.1). (1.6.1-3)

3. We existed before the foundation of the world; since we were going to come into existence through him, we were begotten beforehand by God, and we are the rational creations of the divine Word, through whom we exist from the beginning, because "in the beginning was the Word" (Jn. 1.1). Since the Word existed from the beginning, the Word was, and is the divine source of being for all things. But because the Word has now received the title of Christ, consecrated long ago and worthy of power, I have called the Word the new song. (I.6.4-5)

4. The Word, then, the Christ, caused our existence long ago, for the Word was in God (see Jn. 1.1-2) and is also the

[5]Text of nos. 1-6: GCS, 12³ (1972), 6-10.

cause of our living well; this very same Word has now appeared to human beings (see Tit. 2.11), is alone both God and human, and causes all good things for us. When we have learned from the Word how to live well, then we are ushered into eternal life. This is the new song, the brilliant appearance among us at this time of the Word which existed in the beginning and even before that. The preexistent savior has appeared; the teacher has appeared, the one who exists with existence itself, for "the Word was with God" (Jn. 1.1-2); the Word by whom all things were created has appeared (see Jn. 1.3). As creator the Word gave us life in the beginning at the time of creation; as teacher the Word appeared and taught us how to live well, in order to lead us in the future, as God, to eternal life. Not that the Word took pity on us now for the first time in our wandering; the Word did that right from the very beginning, but appeared in this day, when we were already lost, to save us. (I.7.1, 3-4)

5. The lord, "who, although in the form of God, did not consider equality with God something to be held fast, but emptied himself" (Phil. 2.6-7), will speak to you in person; this is the compassionate God, who longed to save humanity. The Word itself now speaks clearly to you and wins over your lack of faith—the Word of God which became human, so that you could learn from a human being how a human being can become God. (I.8.4)

6. The gates of the Word are rational and are opened by the key of faith. "No one knows God except the Son, and anyone to whom the Son has revealed God" (Mt.11.27). I know well that the one who opened the gate that was closed for so long will reveal hereafter what is within, and will show what until now no one could know, unless they approached through Christ, who alone reveals God. (I.10.3)

7. God's Word is the image of God (see II Cor.4.4); the divine Word is the true Son of Mind, the light that is the original model for light. The image of the Word is the true human being, the mind in the human being, which is, therefore, said to have been made in the image and likeness of God (see Gen. 1.26); this is made like the divine Word by the

intelligence in its heart and is, therefore, rational. (X.98.4)[6]

8. Believe, human beings, in the one who is both human and divine; believe, human beings, in the one who suffered and is worshipped; believe, you who are slaves of death, in the living God; believe, all you human beings, in the one who alone is God of all human beings; believe and receive the reward of salvation. (X.106.4-5)[7]

9. With a speed that cannot be surpassed and with a good will that is open to all, the divine power illuminated the earth and filled everything with the seed of salvation. For the lord did not accomplish such a great task in so short a time without the help of divine providence. The lord was despised for his appearance (see Is. 53.3), but worshipped for his actions; he is purifying, saving, and gentle, the divine Word, who is most clearly true God and who was made equal to the master of everything, because he was his Son, and because the Word was in God (see Jn. 1.1-2). The first proclamation of him in advance of his coming was not met with disbelief, nor did he go unrecognized, when he assumed the role of a human being and fashioned it to flesh for himself, to play out the drama that saved humanity.

For he was a true champion and one who struggled along with the creature. He was diffused very quickly among all people, and, having risen from the will of the Father more quickly than the sun, he shone brightly upon us, bringing in God, through his teachings and the signs he performed, to give testimony about his origin and his identity. He is the Word who brings peace, our mediator and savior; he is the fountain that gives life and peace, and is spread over the whole face of the earth, through whom, so to speak, everything has become a sea of good things. (X.110.1-3)[8]

10. Think for a moment, if you like, about the divine goodness right from the beginning. When the first man was playing freely in the garden, he was still a child of God. But

[6]Text: GCS, 12³ (1972), 71.

[7]Text: GCS, 12³ (1972), 76.

[8]Text: GCS, 12³ (1972), 78.

when he gave in to pleasure, he was seduced by desire; the child grew up in disobedience, refused to obey the father, and was shamed before God. This is the great power of pleasure. The human being who was free because of simple goodness was now bound tight by sins.

The lord wished to free humans from their chains and was, therefore, clothed with flesh, which is a divine mystery in itself; he conquered the serpent, enslaved the tyrant death, and most unexpectedly showed that this human being, who had wandered off to pleasure and been tied down by corruption, was free, with hands untied. O mysterious wonder! The lord lay down, and the human being rose up; the one who fell from the garden receives a greater reward for obedience, namely, heaven. (XI.111.1-3)[9]

The Instructor

11. Our instructor, my children, is like God, his Father, whose Son he is . He is sinless and blameless, and his soul is free of passion; he is God, undefiled, in human form, and minister of the Father's will; he is divine Word, who is in the Father and at the Father's right hand, God with the form of God. He is for us the pure image, and we must try with all our strength to make our souls like him. But he is totally free of human passions, and, therefore, he alone is judge, because he alone is sinless. (I.II.4.1-2)[10]

12. The good instructor, wisdom, the Word of the Father, the one who created the human being, takes care of the whole creature; the all-healing physician of humanity heals both body and soul. (I.II.6.2)[11]

13. Let us, then, give ourselves to the lord, welcoming with great joy this good obedience, holding on to that very strong rope of faith in him, and realizing that virtue means the same for men and women. For if they share one God, then they also have one instructor. They have one church, one moral-

[9]Text: GCS, 12[3] (1972), 78-79.
[10]Text: SC, 70, 114.
[11]Text: SC, 70, 118.

ity, one modesty, and the same form of nourishment; marriage is a common bond, while breathing, seeing, hearing, knowledge, hope, obedience, and love are all the same. Those who share a commmon way of life, grace, and salvation also have a common form of virtue and conduct. Common, therefore, also to men and women is the name of "human being". (I.IV.10.1-3)[12]

14. There is one Father of the universe and one Word of the universe; the Holy Spirit is one and the same everywhere, and there is only one virgin and mother, whom I love to call "church". Alone, this mother did not have milk, for, when alone, she was not a woman; but she is at the same time a virgin and a mother; she is pure as a virgin and full of love as a mother, drawing her children to herself and nursing them with sacred milk, the Word that is meant for infants. She did not have milk, therefore, because the milk was this beautiful child, our kinsman, the body of Christ; she nourished with the Word this young people, whom the lord himself begot with fleshly pain, and whom the lord himself wrapped up in his precious blood. What a holy childbirth! What holy swaddling-clothes! The Word is everything to the infant— father, mother, instructor, and nurse. "Eat my flesh," he says, "and drink my blood" (see Jn. 6.53). Here is the truly good food which the lord provides for us: he offers his flesh and pours out his blood. (I.VI.42.1-3)[13]

15. When he speaks of the flesh, he is speaking to us figuratively about the holy Spirit, for the flesh was made by the holy Spirit. When he says blood, he is speaking to us in images about the Word, since the Word was poured out into life as rich blood. The mixture of both is the lord, the food of the infants; the lord is Spirit and Word. The food, that is, the lord Jesus, who is the Word of God, is Spirit made flesh, heavenly flesh made holy. The food is the Father's milk, on which alone we infants are nursed. The beloved Word in person, our nourisher, shed his own blood for us, therefore,

[12]Text: SC, 70, 128.
[13]Text: SC, 70, 186-188.

to save humanity; through him we believe in God and flee to the Father's care-banishing breast, the Word. He alone, as is proper, provides the milk of love for us infants, and only those are truly blessed who suck on this breast. (I.VI.43.2-4)[14]

16. For Christ the fulfilling of the Father's will was food; for us infants, who drink the Word of heaven like milk, Christ himself is food. In Greek, therefore, one word for seeking comes from the same root as the word for breast, because, to those infants who seek the Word, the Father's breasts, which love humanity, offer milk. (I.VI.46.1)[15]

17. The greatest knowledge of all, it seems, is self-knowledge; for, if one knows oneself, one will also know God, and in knowing God one will be made like God, not by wearing gold or long robes, but by being good and by needing as few things as possible. (III.I.1.1)[16]

18. That person with whom the Word dwells does not vary or change appearance; such a person has the form of the Word, is like God, is beautiful, and is not self-adorned. There is a true beauty, and this is God. That type of person becomes God, since God so wishes it. Heraclitus was right, therefore, to say, "Humans are gods, gods are humans; for it is the same Word[17] in each case." Here is an obvious mystery: God is in a human, the human is God, and the mediator fulfills the Father's will. For the mediator is the Word which is common to both, Son of God and savior of humans, God's servant and our instructor. (III.I.1.5-2.1)[18]

Who is the rich Man who can be saved?

19. What else is necessary? Look at the mysteries of love, and you will see deep into the bosom of the Father, revealed by the one only begotten divine Son. God is love and

[14]Text: SC, 70, 188-190.

[15]Text: SC, 70, 192-194.

[16]Text: SC, 158, 12.

[17]There is a word play here and in the remainder of this passage on the Greek word "Logos," which, in this context, means either "word" or "reason".

[18]Text: SC, 158, 14

appeared to us out of love. In his unspeakable reality God is Father, but out of compassion for us God became Mother. The Father loved and became female, and a great sign of this is the one whom God begot from the very being of God; and the fruit begotten from love is love.

This is why he came down; this why he put on a human being; this is why he willingly underwent human suffering—so that, by adapting himself to our weakness, he might in turn adapt us, whom he loved, to his own power. And when he was about to be poured out as an offering and was giving himself in ransom, he left us a new covenant: I give you my love (see Jn. 13.34). What is this love, and how great is it? For each of us he laid down his life, which was worth as much as all lives; and he demands this of us for one another (see Jn. 15.12-13). (37)[19]

3. ORIGEN

Contra Celsum

1. The gospels knew that the one who said through Jesus, "I am the way, the truth, and the life" (Jn. 14.6) was not limited in any way, which would mean having no existence other than in the soul and body of Jesus; this is clear in many passages, a few of which we shall quote here. When John the baptist prophesies that the Son of God will soon appear, not existing in one particular body and soul, but being present everywhere, he says about him, "There stands in your midst one whom you do not know, who goes before me" (Jn. 1.26-27). If he thought, therefore, that the Son of God was only where the body of Jesus was seen, how could he have said, "There stands in your midst one whom you do not know"? Jesus himself raises the thoughts of his disciples to higher concepts about the Son of God when he says, "Where two or three are gathered together in my name, there I also am in their midst" (Mt. 18.20). This is also the meaning of

[19]Text: GCS, 17², 183-184.

the promise he made to his disciples when he said, "Behold I am with you always until the end of the world" (Mt. 28.20).

In saying this we are not dividing the Son of God from Jesus, for after the incarnation the soul and body of Jesus were united intimately with the Word of God. Paul taught that "the one who was joined to the lord is one spirit" (I Cor. 6.17); if all those who understood the meaning of being joined to the lord and who were actually joined to the lord are indeed one spirit with the lord, then is not that which was once a composite being with the Word of God one with that Word in a more divine and incredible way? (II.9)[20]

2. Let us see how the fictional Jew created by Celsus continues [to object against Christianity]: "If he was so great, then, in order to demonstrate his divinity, he should have disappeared from the cross instantly." It seems to me that this statement resembles the argument of those who oppose divine providence and who picture reality other than it is, saying that it would be better if the world were as we have imagined it. But we want to show that it was not more advantageous for the divine plan as a whole for him to have disappeared instantaneously from the cross in bodily form.

One cannot see in the bare text of the historical account the whole truth of what was written down as having happened to Jesus, for each one of these incidents is revealed as a symbol of something else to those who read the scripture more intelligently. His crucifixion, therefore, contains the truth revealed in the phrase "I am crucified with Christ" (Gal. 2.20), and in the meaning of the words "God forbid that I should boast, except in the cross of my lord Jesus Christ, through whom the world has been crucified to me, and I to the world" (Gal. 6.14); his death was necessary because "as for the death which he died, he died to sin once and for all" (Rom. 6.10), and because the just man says, "being conformed to his death" (Phil. 3.10), and, "For if we die with him, we shall also live with him" (II Tim. 2.11). In the same way, his burial touches those who are conformed to

[20]Text: SC, 132, 304-306.

his death, who were crucified with him, and who died with him, just as Paul also said, "For we were buried with him through baptism" (Rom. 6.4), and we have risen with him. (II.68-69)[21]

3. As for the testimony of the supreme God and of his holy angels, given through the prophets, not after Jesus lived, but before he came to share human existence, do they not move you to marvel at the prophets who received God's Spirit and at the one about whom they prophesied? Neither Jesus nor his disciples wanted the people who came to them to believe only in his divinity and his miracles, as though he did not participate in human nature and had not assumed human flesh, that lusts "against the spirit" (Gal. 5.17); instead, through their faith they saw that the power that came down to human nature and to human circumstances, and that assumed a soul and a human body, was combined with the more sacred realities in order to save believers. The believers see that the divine and human natures began to be interwoven in Jesus, so that the human nature, by its participation in the divine, becomes divine, not only in Jesus, but also in all who, with faith, take up the life which Jesus taught— a life that leads everyone who lives according to Jesus's commands to a loving relationship with God and union with Jesus (III.28)[22]

4. The one whom we think and believe to be God and Son of God from the beginning is the true Word, absolute wisdom, and absolute truth; we say that his mortal body and the human soul that is in him received the highest dignity, not only through fellowship with him, but also through union and blending with him, and that, by participating in his divinity, they were transformed into God. If anyone takes offense at our saying this about his body as well, let that person refer to what the Greeks said about matter: properly speaking matter is without qualities, but it is clothed with whatever qualities the creator wishes to endow it; and it

[21]Text: SC, 132, 444-448.
[22]Text: SC, 136, 66-68.

often puts aside the ones it had, to take on ones that are superior and different. If such ideas are sound, then why is it amazing if the mortal quality of Jesus's body changed into a heavenly and divine quality through the providence of God who willed this? (III.41)[23]

5. It is not to mysteries and to a share in a wisdom "hidden in mystery, which God preordained before the ages for the glory" (I Cor. 2.7) of his just ones that we call the unjust, the thief, the burglar, the poisoner, the sacrilegious, the grave robber, and others like this, whom Celsus might list by way of rhetorical amplification; we call them to healing. For there are qualities in the Word's divinity that help cure those who are sick, about whom the Word said, "It is not those who are well who have need of a doctor, but those who are sick" (Mt. 9.12). There are also other qualities, however, which show to those who are pure in soul and body "the revelation of a mystery which was kept silent through the eternal ages, but was revealed now through the writings of the prophets" (Rom. 16.25-26) and "through the appearance of our lord Jesus Christ" (II Tim. 2.10); this appearance is revealed to each of the perfect, and enlightens their minds to a true knowledge of reality. The divine Word was sent as a physician to the sinners, but as a teacher of divine mysteries to those who were already pure and who no longer sinned. (III.61-62)[24]

6. For some reason or other Celsus also criticizes us for saying that "God himself will come down to humans," for he thinks that, as a result of this, "he abandoned his throne." He does not know the power of God and "that the lord's Spirit has filled the world and that which holds everything together knows all that is said" (Wis. 1.7); and he cannot understand the words, "Do I not fill heaven and earth, says the lord?" (Jer. 23.24). He does not see that, according to Christian teaching, all of us "live and move and have our being in him" (Acts 17.28), as Paul taught in his discourse to

[23]Text: SC, 136, 96-98.
[24]Text: SC, 136, 140-142.

the Athenians. And so, even if the God of the universe, by his own power, comes down through Jesus into human life, and even if the Word, who was "in the beginning with God" and himself "was God" (Jn. 1.1-2), comes to us, he does not change places or leave his throne, as though one place were without him, and another, which did not possess him before, were now full of him. The power and divinity of God come to live here through the one whom God chooses and in whom God finds room, without God's changing places or leaving one place empty of God's presence and another filled with it.

Even if we do say that God leaves one place and fills another, we do not mean this in the sense of physical space. We would say that the soul of a wicked person immersed in evil is abandoned by God, and we would assert that the soul of a person who wishes to live virtuously, or is progressing in this type of life, or is even living in this way already, is filled with, or shares in a divine Spirit. For Christ to descend, therefore, or for God to turn toward humans, it is not necessary to abandon a throne on high or to change things here, as Celsus thinks, when he says, "If you change even one insignificant thing on earth, everything will be overturned and destroyed." But if you must say that certain things change because of the presence of God's power and because of the coming of the Word to humans , we shall not hesitate to say that those who have opened their souls to the coming of God's Word change from bad to good, from licentiousness to moderation, and from superstition to true religion.

But if you want us to pay attention to even the silliest of Celsus's attacks, listen to what he says: "Suppose that God was not known by human beings and, therefore, felt that he lacked the proper honor; would God want to make himself known and to test both believers and unbelievers, in the way that people who have recently come into great wealth wish to show off? This is an intense and very mortal lust for honor that they are ascribing to God." We say in reply that God, who is not known by bad people, would desire to be known, not because God feels a lack of the proper honor, but because knowledge of God frees the knower from misfortune. And it is not because of a desire to "test both believers and unbelievers" that God either dwells in some through an ineffable, divine power, or sends his Christ; God does this, so that believers might possess God's divinity and be freed from misfortune, and that unbelievers might no longer be able to excuse their lack of belief on the pretext that they did not hear or were not taught.

What argument, therefore, supports the claim that it follows that God, in our teaching, is like people with newly acquired wealth who wish to show off? God does not wish to show off before us, because God desires us to understand and perceive the divine supremacy; what God wants is to implant in us the blessedness that arises in our souls from knowing God, and, therefore, strives to bring it about that we obtain an intimate relationship with God through Christ and the continuous coming of the Word. Christian teaching, therefore, ascribes no mortal lust for honor to God. (IV.5-6)[25]

7. What came down to humans was originally "in the form of God" (Phil. 2.6), and out of love for humanity "emptied himself" (Phil. 2.7), so that humans could receive him. In no way did he undergo a change from good to evil, for "he committed no sin" (I Pt. 2.22), nor did he go from beauty to shame, since "he knew no sin" (II Cor. 5.21); he did not go from happiness to misfortune, but rather "humbled himself" (Phil. 2.8) and was nonetheless happy, even when he humbled himself to the advantage of our race. Furthermore he did not go through a change from the best to the most evil; for how can goodness and love of humanity be most evil? This would be just like saying that the physician, who sees horrible things and touches disgusting things, in order to cure sick people, goes from good to bad, from beauty to shame, or from happiness to misfortune; and yet the physician, who sees horrible things and touches disgusting things, cannot totally escape the possibility of falling into the same state.

[25]Text: SC, 136, 196-202.

But the one who cures the wounds of our souls, through the divine Word in him, was absolutely incapable of evil. If, however, the immortal divine Word assumed a mortal body and a human soul, and seems, therefore, to Celsus to undergo a change or tranformation, let him learn that the Word remains Word in substance; for the Word suffers none of the changes undergone by body or soul, but comes down at times to the one who cannot look at the radiance and splendor of the Word's divinity, becomes, as it were, flesh, and is expressed in the form of a body, until the one who has received the Word in this way has been slowly lifted up by it and can gaze upon what I would call its primary form.

The Word has, so to speak, different forms, for it appears to each one of those who are led to a knowledge of it in a manner corresponding to the state of the one who is being led; this depends on whether the person has advanced a little or a great deal, is already close to virtue, or established in it. Our God, therefore, was not transformed in the way that Celsus and those like him understand this, and, when he went up "to the high mountain" (Mt. 17.21), he showed his own form, which was different from, and far greater than the one seen by those who remained below, because they could not follow him on high. For those who remained below did not have eyes which were capable of seeing the transformation of the Word into something glorious and more divine; they could scarcely take him in as he was, and, therefore, those who were unable to look at his higher state could say about him, "We have seen him, and he had neither form nor beauty, but his form was without honor, most desolate of the sons of men" (Is. 53.2-3). Let this, then, be our answer to the ideas of Celsus, who understood neither the changes and transformations of Jesus that were described in the accounts, nor the fact that his status was both mortal and immortal.

If [Celsus] had comprehended the fate of a soul that will live with eternal life, and had acquired a correct understanding of its substance and origin, he would not have mocked in this way the concept of the immortal entering a mortal body (I do not mean Plato's transmigration of souls, but a different, more exalted explanation of this phenomenon). He would also have been aware of one special descent, done out of a deep love of humanity, to bring back, as sacred scripture in a mystical sense calls them, "the lost sheep of the house of Israel" (Mt. 15.24), who had gone down away from the mountains, and toward whom the shepherd is said in some parables to have descended, leaving behind on the mountain the sheep who had not strayed (see Mt. 18.12-13 and parallels).

One's response [to Celsus's arguments based on the question of changes in God] would deal, on the one hand, with the nature of the divine Word, who is God, and with the soul of Jesus on the other. With respect to the nature of the Word, therefore, one would say this: the quality of food in the nursing mother changes into milk to suit the nature of the infant; food is also prepared by a physician to render it useful for restoring the health of a sick person, or it is adapted to the needs of a stronger person who can take it as it is. In the same way, according to what each one deserves, God changes for human beings the power of the Word, which by nature nourishes the human soul. For one he becomes, as scripture called it, "genuine spiritual milk" (I Pt. 2.2); to a second, weaker person he is like a vegetable (Rom. 14.2), while to one who is perfect "solid food" is given (see Heb. 5.12 and 14). The Word is surely not untrue to its own nature in providing each one with nourishment adapted to one's receptive capacity; in doing this the Word does not deceive or lie.

As for the soul of Jesus, if one assumes that it changed when it entered a body, we shall ask how one defines change. If it means change of substance, we disagree, not only in this case, but in that of every other rational soul as well. If it means that it suffers something from being united to the body, or from the place to which it has come, then why is it considered strange for the Word, out of a deep love for humanity, to bring down a savior for the human race? Nobody who in the past promised to cure people was able to do as much as this soul proclaimed by its actions, even descending willingly into human weakness for the sake of our race. This is the divine Word's thought, which is expressed in many scriptural passages. It is enough for now to present the following statement from Paul.

> Let this thought be in you, which was also in Christ Jesus, who, being in the form of God, did not judge being equal to God something that had to be tightly grasped; instead, he emptied himself and took the form of a slave; having been found in appearance as human, he humbled himself, becoming obedient unto death, even to the death of the cross. God has, therefore, exalted him and given him a name which is above every other name (Phil. 2.5-9). (IV.15-18)[26]

8. Celsus approves of people who, in keeping with certain traditions, worship crocodiles and treat them with honor, and he has not written one word against them. But he feels that Christians should be censured for learning, on the one hand, to despise evil and to avoid actions which arise from it, and, on the other, to show reverence and respect for virtue, because it springs from God and is a Son of God. For we must not think that wisdom and righteousness are female in substance, because the words for them are female in gender; we believe that the Son of God is these things, as his authentic disciple declared when he said about him, "Who was begotten for us from God as wisdom, righteousness, sanctification, and redemption" (I Cor. 1.30). Even if we call him a second God, therefore, let everyone know that "second God" means nothing except the virtue which comprises all virtues, and the Word which encompasses every single word of the beings created according to nature, whether they be primary beings or ones created for the good of the whole. We say that this Word dwelt in, and was united to the soul of Jesus more intimately than in any other soul, since he alone was able to sustain perfectly total participation in the absolute Word,

[26]Text: SC, 136, 218-228.

absolute wisdom and absolute justice. (V.39)[27]

9. It is not remarkable if, after saying that the soul of Jesus was united to the glorious Son of God through total participation in him, we make no other distinction between the soul and the Son. For the sacred words of divine scripture are aware of other realities which are two in their natures, but which are considered to become one with each other, and actually are so. It was said about husband and wife, for example, that "they are no longer two, but one flesh" (Gen. 2.24; Mt. 19.6); about the one who was both perfect and joined to the true lord, Word, wisdom, and truth it was said, "the one who is joined to the lord is one spirit" (I Cor. 6.17). If, then, "the one who is joined to the lord is one spirit," who, other than the soul of Jesus, is more, or even comparably united to the lord, the absolute Word, absolute wisdom, absolute truth, and absolute justice? If this is so, then the soul of Jesus and the "firstborn of all creation" (see Col. 1.15), the divine Word, are not related as two separate realities.

Celsus does not laugh at or ridicule the teaching of the Stoic philosophers, who say that humans and God have the same virtue, and that the god of all is no happier than the one human being whom they consider wise, for both are equally happy; but if divine scripture states that the perfect man is joined by virture and united to the Word itself, so that we conclude from this that we cannot separate the soul of Jesus from "the firstborn of all creation" (see Col. 1.15), he laughs at the statement that Jesus is Son of God; he does not understand what was said about him in divine scripture in a secret and mystical way.

We state that the divine scriptures say that the body of Christ, which is given life by the Son of God, is the whole church of God, and that the limbs of this body, taken as a whole, are any and all believers. A soul gives life to, and moves the body which, of its nature, does not make vital movements of itself; in the same way, the Word, which

[27]Text: SC, 147, 118-220.

moves and actuates the whole body to do what is necessary, moves the church and each limb of the members of the church, which does nothing apart for the Word. If this point has, as I think, a logic that is not to be despised, why is it difficult to believe that the soul of Jesus, or, quite simply, Jesus himself, because of the total and unsurpassable union with the Word itself, is not separated from the only-begotten and "firstborn of all creation" (see Col. 1.15), and is in no way distinct from it? (VI.47-48)[28]

10. If Celsus asks us "how we think we shall know God, and how we suppose we shall be saved by him," we shall answer that the Word of God, which comes to those who seek it or who received it when it appeared, is quite capable of making known and revealing the Father, who was not visible before the coming of the Word. Who else but the divine Word can save and lead the human soul to the God of all? The Word was "in the beginning with God" (Jn. 1.1), but for the sake of those who were joined to the flesh and became as flesh, he "became flesh" (Jn. 1.14), so that he might be comprehended by those who could not see him insofar as he was "Word," and was "with God," and "was God" (Jn. 1.1). Spoken of in terms of the body and proclaimed as flesh, he calls to himself those who are flesh, to cause them to be formed in the likeness of the Word who became flesh, and then to raise them up to see him as he was before he became flesh. He did this so that they could receive help and could rise up from the initial stage of the flesh to say, "If we have ever known Christ according to the flesh, now we no longer know him in this way" (II Cor. 5.16). "He became flesh," therefore, and having become flesh, "he dwelt among us" (Jn. 1.14) and was not apart from us. As he dwelt among us and was in our midst, he did not remain in his primary form, but led us up to the spiritual "high mountain," and showed us his glorious form and the radiance of his clothing—and not only of himself alone, but also of the spiritual law, that is, Moses, who was seen in glory with

[28]Text: SC, 147, 298-300.

Jesus. He also showed us all prophecy, which did not die after he became human, but was raised up into heaven; and the symbol of this was Elijah (see Mt. 17.1-3). (VI.68)[29]

11. Insofar as [Jesus] was a human being, adorned more than every other human being with total participation in the absolute Word and absolute wisdom, he endured, as a wise and perfect person, whatever a person had to endure who was doing everything on behalf of the whole human race and of rational beings. There is nothing extraordinary in the fact that the human being died, and that his death not only was an example of dying for religion, but also started and advanced the destruction of the evil one, the devil, who ruled over the whole earth (see Heb. 2.14-15; I Jn. 5.19; Rev. 12.9). Signs of the evil one's deposition are the people everywhere who, through the coming of Jesus, have escaped from the demons who held them captive, and who, because they were freed from subjugation to those demons, have dedicated themselves to God and to a devotion to God, which, in proportion to their power, becomes more pure every day. (VII.17)[30]

[29]Text: SC, 147, 348-350.
[30]Text: SC, 150, 52.

Chapter Four

Fourth Century Greek Writers

I. Introduction

Early in the fourth century an Alexandrian priest named Arius was accused of teaching that the Word of God, the second member of the Christian trinity, was a creature and not truly divine. Many of his contemporaries felt that such a belief destroyed Christian faith and rendered invalid the salvation promised through Jesus Christ, the Word become flesh. Others, however, supported Arius, and the fierce controversy that arose over his ideas split the Christian community into numerous factions; its effects were felt into the fifth century and even beyond, despite the fact that he and his alleged teaching were condemned by a general synod, or council, of the Christian church, which met in the city of Nicaea, at the behest of the emperor Constantine, in the year 325. Recent literature has questioned the accuracy of the judgement passed on Arius by his own contemporaries and by later generations of Christians; whatever the outcome of the current discussion, however, what is important here is, not the validity of his peers' perception of Arius, but the conceptual content of their responses to him.

One of the most outspoken and famous critics of Arius was Athanasius (d. 373), who was bishop of Alexandria for over forty years. He devoted his life to combatting a teaching that he saw as a deadly heresy, and experienced a series of victories and defeats, depending on whether the good will of the political powers favored either Arius or himself. In responding to Arius, Athanasius stressed the full divinity of God's word and the reality of the flesh with which that Word appeared in this world. For him, if a truly divine Word did not really become flesh, then Jesus Christ, the Word become flesh, could not save humanity from the power of sin and death. His concerns and the manner in which he links salvation to the person of the Word become flesh appear clearly in quotations from two of his letters.

The influence of ideas stemming from Arius and his supporters did not diminish after the council of Nicaea, and the fourth century was more than half over before the various parties of mainstream orthodox Christians reached a modicum of agreement on how to express their faith in the divinity of the word become flesh. The holy Spirit came under scrutiny next, and was finally declared as divine as the other members of the Christian trinity at a council held in Constantinople in the year 381. The major theological quest during this era was the search for a means of explaining how three realities, called Father, Son, and holy Spirit, could be truly divine and somehow distinct, without destroying the monotheism that was at the heart of the Judaeo-Christian tradition. Leaders in this task were three bishops from Cappadocia, a region that lies in present-day Turkey.

Basil of Caesarea (d. 379), his brother Gregory of Nyssa (d. 395), and their friend Gregory of Nazianzus (d. 389) were concerned primarily with trinitarian theology; but, as Christian teachers, they also had to think and speak about the Word become flesh and about the salvation that this person, Jesus Christ, brought. All of them stressed the divinity of the Word and their belief that, by becoming human, the Word enabled humanity to participate in that divinity—a process known as divinization. The Word become flesh was, therefore, seen as revealer of God and redeemer, or savior; but their unanimity on the basic concepts did not extend to all areas of concern.

Gregory of Nyssa approached redemption in a naive way that was not uncommon in the early church; he believed that the devil had a right, because of sin, to enslave humanity, and that it would, accordingly, have been unjust for God simply to put an end to that captivity by an act of the will. Through the humanity, which hid the divinity of the Word become flesh, God, therefore, tricked the devil into committing an injustice by seizing, through death, an innocent person, Jesus Christ; because of this crime the devil lost all power, and humanity was freed from the power of sin and death. Gregory of Nazianzus flatly rejected this theory as unworthy of God, and, for the same reason, refused to consider Christ's death as a kind of peace offering which soothed God's anger.

In another area, that of the relationship between the divinity and the humanity of Jesus Christ, the two Gregorys again seem to diverge. Gregory of Nyssa spoke of an apparently ongoing, dynamic perfecting of the humanity of Christ through the divinity, in terms similar to those used in a later generation by Theodore of Mopsuestia.[1] Gregory of Nazianzus favored a more static approach, which emphasized the dominant role of the divinity. They both agreed, therefore, about the need for the divinization of the human, in imitation of what happened to the humanity of Jesus, but not about the nature of the process.

Gregory of Nazianzus stated clearly that salvation, like sin, is the same for the male and the female, who should be equal partners in all aspects of Christian life. Most of the writers quoted in this volume would probably have agreed with this statement in principle, but only Gregory of Nazianzus actually formulated the thought in writing.

Diversity of thought and expression flourished, therefore, as late as the fourth century, in writers of unquestionable

---

[1]Theodore is discussed in the final chapter. His orthodoxy, unlike that of Gregory, did not go unchallenged.

orthodoxy, whose theology, for its time, was complex and not unsophisticated. Mainstream Christianity was indeed monolithic in its opposition to the Arian tradition, but it discovered a remarkable variety of forms to express that negative reaction.

John Chrysostom (d. 407), who was a renowned preacher,[2] was born in Antioch in Syria, served as a priest there, and became bishop of Constantinople, the capital city and home of the emperor. Although he was actively engaged in ministry during the height of the Apollinarian controversy,[3] he seems to have been primarily concerned with Arianism. He stressed the divinity of the Word, therefore, and understood its becoming flesh as a *datum* of faith, which was simply to be believed without philosophical analysis; salvation, for him, as a sign of God's ineffable love for humanity, was to be approached with the same attitude. In numerous homilies he expressed the faith, not of the theologians or controversialists, but of the people, and for this reason he is often described as unoriginal or uninteresting. The final judgement on this question depends on the judge's point of view, but there is little doubt that Chrysostom is an eloquent witness to the faith of his day.

It is instructive, then, to compare Chrysostom's thought with that of Theodore of Mopsuestia (d. 428), a contemporary and friend of his youth, and with the early work of Cyril of Alexandria (d. 444),[4] who was younger than Chrysostom and who attacked Chrysostom after his death. Chrysostom is far closer to Cyril, as he wrote before the start of the Nestorian controversy, than he is to Theodore, who was trained in the same tradition as Chrysostom, but who became a focus of intense controversy after his death.

[2]"Chrysostom" is a nickname meaning "the man with the golden mouth."

[3]See the final chapter for further details.

[4]See the final chapter on these two authors; Cyril's early thought can be found in his commentary on the gospel of John.

II. The Writings

1. ATHANASIUS

Letter to Adelphius[5]

1. We have read what your reverence wrote, and we truly approve of your piety toward Christ; we give glory in the first place to the God who bestowed such great grace on you that you can think correctly and be aware, as far as possible, of the devil's deceits. At the same time, we are astounded at the wickedness of the heretics, seeing that they have fallen so far into the pit of impiety, that they can no longer maintain their good sense, but are totally corrupt in their thinking. First of all, they denied the divinity of the only begotten Son of God, but pretended to acknowledge that he came in the flesh; now, however, having gradually drifted into decline and having abandoned this opinion, they have simply become unbelievers. As a result they cannot acknowledge the very existence of God and cannot believe that God became human. You should teach them that they are following the ideas of Valentinus, Marcion, and Manichaeus, some of whom substituted appearance for reality, while others divided the indivisible and denied that "the Word became flesh and dwelt among us" (Jn. 1.14). (1-2)

2. We do not worship a creature; that would be impossible. This kind of error is pagan or Arian. We worship the lord of creation, the Word of God become flesh. For even if the flesh in itself is a part of creation, it has nonetheless become God's body. We do not divide the body from the Word and worship it by itself, nor, in our desire to worship the Word, do we separate it from the flesh. Knowing, as we just said, that "the Word became flesh," we acknowledge this Word to be God, even after it has come into being in flesh.

Who, therefore, would be so stupid as to say to the lord, "Step aside from your body, so that I can worship you"?

[5]Text: PG, 26.1072-1084.

Who is so wicked as to join the Jews of the gospel in saying to him, because of the body, "Why do you, who are human, make yourself God?" (Jn. 10.33)? The leper was not like this, for he worshipped the God who was in a body and knew that it was God; he said, "If you wish, lord, you can make me clean" (Mt. 8.2). He did not think that, because of the flesh, the Word of God, was a creature; nor, because the Word was the author of all creation, did he despise the flesh with which the Word had been clothed. He worshipped the creator of the universe as though in a created temple, and he was made clean. The woman with the hemorrhage, who believed and merely touched the fringe of his garment, was cured in the same way (Mt. 9.20-22); the sea with its foaming waves heard the Word become flesh, and the storm ceased (Mt. 8.26); the man who was blind from birth was cured by the Word through some fleshly spittle (Jn. 9.6ff.). And, finally, there is something greater and even more remarkable, which would perhaps have shocked even the most irreligious people: when the lord was hanging on the cross—it was his body, and the Word was in it—the sun darkened, the earth shook, the stones split open, the curtain in the temple was torn, and many bodies of holy people who had died arose (see Mt. 27.51-52; Lk. 23.45). (3)

3. This happened, but no one debated, as the Arians dare to do in these days, about whether or not one should believe in the Word become flesh. As a matter of fact, although they were looking at a human being, they acknowledged him to be their creator; when they heard a human voice, they did not, because of the human aspect, say that the Word is a creature. On the contrary, they trembled in awe and knew clearly that the voice was coming from a sacred temple. How can the wicked, therefore, not be afraid that, "since they did not decide to keep God in their minds, they would be handed over to wicked thoughts, to do things that they should not do" (see Rom. 1.28)? For creation does not worship a creature, nor, on the other hand, did it, because of the flesh, refuse to worship its lord; it saw its maker in a body, and "at the name of Jesus Christ every knee bent and will bend, of

those in heaven, on earth, and under the earth; and every tongue will confess," even if the Arians disapprove, "that Jesus Christ is lord to the glory of God the Father" (Phil. 2.10-11).

For the flesh did not bring dishonor on the Word; we would never say that. Instead, the flesh was glorified by the Word. Nor did the divinity of the Son diminish, when the Son, who was in the form of God, assumed the form of a slave (see Phil. 2.6-7); the Son became the liberator of all flesh and of all creation (see Rom. 8.21). And if God sent his Son born of a woman, this fact brings to us, not shame, but rather glory and great grace (see Gal. 4.4). For he became human to make us gods through himself; he came into being through a woman and was born of a virgin, in order to change our sinful form of birth into himself, so that we might become a holy people and "share in the divine nature," as the blessed Peter wrote (II Pt. 1.4). "What was impossible for the law, since it was weak because of the flesh, God [did], sending his only Son in the likeness of the flesh of sin and for sin, and he condemned sin in the flesh" (Rom. 8.3). (4)

4. The people who despise the flesh assumed by the Word in order to free all human beings, to raise them all from the dead, and to deliver them from sin, and those who, because of the flesh, accuse the Son of God of being a mere creature, certainly appear to be ungrateful and deserving of utter contempt; for they all but cry out to God and say, "Do not send your only-begotten Son in flesh; do not make him take flesh from a virgin, lest he free us from death and sin. We do not want him to come into existence with a body, lest he should undergo death for us. We do not want the Word to become flesh, lest through the flesh he should become the mediator of our approaching you, and we should come to inhabit dwelling places in heaven. Let the gates of heaven remain closed, lest your Word, through the veil of its flesh, consecrate the road to heaven for us." Here are their words, expressed with a satanic boldness that caused them to devise this perversity for themselves. Those who do not wish to worship the Word become flesh show no gratitude for its

becoming human; those who separate the Word from the flesh do not believe that one liberation from sin and one destruction of death took place. Where in the world will these wicked people find the flesh assumed by the savior all by itself, so that they dare to say, "We do not worship the lord with the flesh; we divide the body from the lord and worship the lord alone"?

Blessed Stephen saw the lord standing at the right hand [of God] in heaven (see Acts 7.55), and angels said to the disciples, "He will come in the same way that you saw him going into heaven" (Acts 1.11). The lord himself spoke to the Father and said, "I desire that, where I am, they too will always be with me" (Jn. 17.24). If the flesh, therefore, cannot be divided from the Word, then these people must surely lay aside their error and worship the Father in the name of our lord Jesus Christ; or, if they will not worship and will not serve the Word become flesh, then they must definitely be rejected by everybody and no longer be considered Christians. (5)

5. This, as we have just described it, is the bold insanity of those people. But our faith is correct; it flows from the teaching of the apostles and the tradition of the fathers, and is confirmed by the new and old covenants. For the prophets say, "Send forth your word and your truth" (Ps 43.3), and, "Behold the young woman will conceive and will bear a son, and they will call his name Emmanuel, which means 'God is with us'" (Is. 7.14). And what else does this mean but that God has come into being through flesh? The apostolic tradition teaches, in the words of blessed Peter, that "Christ suffered for us in flesh" (I Pt. 4.1); Paul writes, "Waiting for the blessed hope and appearance of the glory of our mighty God and savior Jesus Christ, who gave himself for us, to deliver us from all sin, and to purify for himself a people of his own, eager to do good works" (Tit. 2.13-14). How could he have given himself for us, then, if he did not have flesh? For he offered the flesh and gave himself for us, so that, by undergoing death in the flesh, he might crush the devil, who controlled the power of death.

Let us, therefore, always give thanks in the name of Jesus Christ, and let us not reject the grace which comes to us through him. For the coming of the savior in the flesh was both the ransom paid for death and the salvation of all creation. And so, dearly beloved, let those who love the lord be reminded by what I say here; as for those who have imitated Judas and abandoned the lord to follow Caiaphas, let them learn a better way from these words. They only have to be willing, and to feel shame. Let them understand that, in worshipping the lord in flesh, we are not worshipping a creature, but rather, as we have explained, the creator clothed with a created body. (6)

6. I would like your reverence to ask them this. When Israel was ordered to go up to Jerusalem to worship in the lord's temple, where the ark, and over it the cherubim of glory who overshadowed the mercy-seat, were to be found, did they perform a good act or the opposite? If they were acting badly, why were those who scorned this law subject to punishment? For it was written that anyone who shows scorn and does not go up will be removed from among the people (see Lev. 17.9). If, on the other hand, they were acting well and became pleasing to God in this way, then why do the Arians, those abominable and most shameful heretics, not deserve to be destroyed many times over? For they approve of the ancient people because of the honor they pay the temple, but are unwilling to worship the lord who is in flesh as in a temple.

The old temple was made of stone and decorated with gold, and was like a shadow; but when the reality came, then the image came to an end, and, as the lord said, "there did not remain in it stone upon stone, which was not torn down" (see Mt. 24.2). When they looked at the temple made of stones, they did not think that the lord who spoke in the temple was a creature, nor did they despise the temple and go far away to worship; they went into it and gave proper service to the God who spoke from the temple. Since this was so, how can one fail to worship the lord's body, which is truly all-holy and all-sacred, and which was announced by

the archangel Gabriel, formed by the holy Spirit (see Lk.
1.26-35), and became the garment of the Word? It was a
bodily hand that the Word stretched out to raise the woman
suffering from a fever (see Mk. 1.30-31), and he spoke a
human word to raise Lazarus from the dead (see Jn. 11.43).
Stretching out his hands again on the cross, he overthrew
"the ruler of the power of the air, who works now in the sons
of disobedience" (Eph. 2.2), and gave us a clear path to
heaven. (7).

7. The person who despises the temple, therefore, despises
the lord who is in the temple, while the one who separates
the Word from the body, rejects the grace given to us
through the Word. And these wicked Arian maniacs should
not think that, because the body is created, the Word too is a
creature, nor should they misrepresent the Word's body
because the Word is not a creature. Let them listen. If the
Word were a creature, it would not have assumed the created
body, in order to give it life. For what help can creatures
receive from a creature which needs salvation itself? But
since the Word itself is creator and maker of creatures, it put
on created reality at the end of time, so that it could, as
creator, renew and restore creation once again. A creature
could not be saved by a creature, just as creatures could not
be created by a creature, if the Word was not creator.

Let them, therefore, stop lying about the divine scriptures
and scandalizing simple Christians. If they are willing, let
them change their minds and stop serving the creature
instead of the God who created everything. But if they wish
to persevere in their wickedness, let them feed on it by themselves and gnash their teeth like their father, the devil. For
the faith of the universal church knows that the Word of
God is creator and maker of all things, and we know that "In
the beginning was the Word, and the Word was with God"
(Jn. 1.1). And we worship the Word that became human for
our salvation, not as one who became an equal in an equal
body, but as the lord who assumed the form of the slave (see
Phil. 2.7), and as the maker and creator who came into
existence as a creature, so that he might free everything

through that creature, present the universe to the Father, and give peace to all things, in heaven and on earth (see Col. 1.20). For in this way we acknowledge the divinity he shares with the Father, and worship his presence in the flesh. (8)

Letter to Maximus[6]

8. Athanasius sends greetings in the lord to his most dearly beloved son, Maximus the philosopher. I have read your recent letter and I approve of your piety; I had planned to keep absolute silence, since I was rather shocked at the audacity of people who simply do not understand what they are teaching or talking about. Responding when the issues are so obvious that they are clearer than light merely provides such lawless people with a pretext for acting wickedly. I waited for some time, therefore, and, when I saw how eager for battle these shameless people were, I gave in to your zeal for the truth and replied, but only to your letter, so that our enemies might be persuaded on those points which they contradicted. But if they are not overcome with shame under these circumstances, then keep in mind the apostle's command: "After a first and second admonition, avoid a person who is factious, for you know that such a person is perverted and a sinner, and stands self-condemned" (Tit. 3.10-11). If these people pretend to be Christians, let them know that the crucified Christ is "lord of glory" (see I Cor. 2.8), "power of God and wisdom of God" (see I Cor. 1.24). (1)

9. If they doubt that he is God, let them show respect for Thomas, who touched the crucified one and said that he was lord and God (see Jn. 20.28). And let them show reverence for the lord himself, who, after washing the disciples' feet, said, "You call me lord and teacher and you say well, for that is what I am" (Jn. 13.13). He carried our sins up onto the tree with the same body that was his when he washed their feet (see I Pt. 2.24). He was acknowledged as lord of creation through the testimony of the sun drawing back its rays, of

[6]Text: PG, 26.1085-1089.

the earth trembling, of the rocks splitting open, and of the executioners confessing that the one crucified was truly Son of God (see Mt. 27.51-54; Mk. 15.39; Lk. 23.44-45). For the body they saw was not the body of some human being, but of God; and, since God was in that body, when he was crucified, he raised the dead. An evil thing, therefore, is their boldness in saying that the Word of God came into some holy man; for that is what happened with all the prophets and other holy people. This, however, is absolutely impossible and unthinkable. But "the Word became flesh" (Jn. 1.14), "once and for all at the end time for the abolition of sin" (Heb. 9.26); he came forth from the virgin Mary, a human being in our likeness (see Phil. 2.7); as he said to the Jews, "Why do you seek to kill me, a human being who has spoken the truth to you?" (Jn. 8.40). We are made divine, not by participation in the body of some human being, but by receiving the body of the Word itself. (2).

10. I am also amazed that they would dare to believe that his becoming human was quite simply natural. If that were so, then all mention of Mary would be superfluous; for nature knows nothing of a virgin giving birth without a man's being involved. Because of the Father's will, therefore, he was true God, Word by nature, and wisdom of the Father; he became a human being with a true body for the sake of our salvation, so that, having something to offer for us (see Heb. 8.3), he might save all of us, who "through fear of death were subject to slavery for our whole life long" (Heb. 2.15). For it was not merely some human being who gave himself up for us, since every human being is subject to death, in accordance with the words that were said to all through Adam, "You are earth and to earth you shall return" (Gen. 3.19); nor was it some other creature, since all creation is subject to change. No, it was the Word itself which offered its own body for us, so that our faith and hope might not rest on a human being, but that we might have faith in the divine Word itself.

When the Word becomes human, we see its glory, "glory as of an only begotten son from a father, full of grace and truth"(see Jn. 1.14). For as God he gave glory to all that he suffered through the body. Through flesh he was hungry, but as God he fed those who were hungry. Anyone who is offended by the bodily reality should believe because of the actions of God. As a human being, he found out where Lazarus had been placed; but it was through divine power that he raised him. No one should, therefore, laugh and say that he is a child, pointing to his age, growth, eating, drinking, and suffering; for if one denies the properties of his body, one might deny absolutely his presence among us. But just as his becoming human was not simply natural, it was, on the other hand, quite right for him, after assuming a body, to display its properties, so that the illusory incarnation taught by Manichaeus might not prevail. At the same time, when he was acting with the body, it was also proper for him not to conceal the reality of his divinity, lest Paul of Samosata find some excuse for saying that he is indeed human, but also another person distinct from the divine Word. (3).

11. Let the unbeliever see all this, therefore, and learn that he was an infant in a crib, but was worshipped by the Magi and made them subject to him; that he came down to Egypt as a child, but rendered idolatry's artifacts impotent; that he was crucified in the flesh, but raised dead bodies that had been rotting for a long time. And it became clear to everyone that he endured everything, not for himself, but for us, so that we, through his suffering, might be clothed with incorruptibility and the power not to suffer, so that we might live eternal life. (4).

2. The Cappadocians

A. BASIL OF CAESAREA

Letter 261 — To the People of Sozopolis[7]

1. You wrote that there are people among you who destroy, insofar as they can, the saving work of our lord Jesus Christ, by rejecting the grace of the great mystery which was shrouded in silence from the beginning of time, but revealed in our own time (see Rom. 16.25-26), when the lord, after going through everything needed for the care of the human race, gave us the grace, in addition to everything else, of his own coming. In the last days he was himself revealed in the flesh, "born of a woman, born subject to the law, to redeem those who were subject to the law, so that we might receive adoption as true children" (Gal. 4.4-5). (1)

2. If the lord's coming in the flesh did not take place, then, the redeemer did not pay to death the price of our redemption, nor did he put an end to death's reign through himself. For, if one thing was subject to death, but something else was assumed by the lord, death would never have stopped doing its work, and the sufferings of the flesh that bore God would have been of no benefit to us; he would not have killed sin through the flesh, and we who had died through Adam would not have been given life through Christ; what had fallen apart would not have been created anew, that which had been shattered would not have been restored, and that which had been alienated through the serpent's deceit would not have been brought into a new relationship with God. All these benefits are destroyed by those who say that the lord came with a heavenly body. What need was there of the holy virgin, if the flesh that bore Christ was not going to be assumed from the clay of Adam? (2)

3. Statements which claim that human changes touch the divinity itself come either from people who think illogically or from those who are unaware that movements of flesh,

[7]Text: *Saint Basile. Lettres,* ed. Yves Courtonne, III, 116-118.

movements of flesh animated by a soul, and movements of a soul using a body are all different realities. Being cut, becoming smaller, and being dissolved are properties of flesh; growing weary, and experiencing pain, hunger, and thirst are properties of flesh animated by a soul; feeling grief, distress, care, and similar emotions are properties of a soul using a body. Some of these movements are natural and even necessary for the living being; others are products of an evil will and are introduced in addition to the others because of a way of life that is dissolute and devoid of training in virtue.

It is clear, therefore, that the lord assumed the natural movements to establish the fact that he became human in a real way, and not through some imaginary process; but he rejected as unworthy of the undefiled divinity the passions that spring from evil and befoul the purity of our lives. He is, therefore, said to have come into being "in the likeness of the flesh of sin" (Rom. 8.3). Although he assumed our flesh with its natural movements, therefore, he did not commit sin (see 1 Pet. 2.22). Just as death, which was transmitted to us in flesh through Adam, was, however, swallowed by the divinity, so sin too was utterly destroyed by the righteousness which is in Christ Jesus, so that, in the resurrection, we receive back a flesh that is not subject to death or liable to sin. (3)

B. GREGORY OF NYSSA

Oratio Catechetica[8]

1. What, then, is justice in this case? It consists in not exercising any kind of arbitrary power against the one who controls us, and in not tearing us away through excessive force from the one who holds us, so as to avoid supplying a pretext for a just complaint to the one who enslaved humanity through pleasure. Those who have sold their freedom for

---

[8]Text: *The Catechetical Oration of Gregory of Nyssa*, ed. by James Herbert Srawley, 84-93.

money are slaves of the people who bought them, and neither they nor anyone else may invoke freedom as an aid on their behalf, even if those who sold themselves into this condition belong to noble families. A person who employs force against the buyer out of concern for the one who has bartered himself away will clearly be seen as unjust, for freeing through the use of arbitrary force one who had been legally purchased. But if someone wishes to repurchase such a person, there is no law against that. In the same way, since we had voluntarily bartered ourselves away, a just method of restoration, not an arbitrary one, had to be devised by the one who through goodness was setting us free again. This means that one must give the one in control the whole ransom desired in exchange for the captive. (22).

2. What, then, was the one in control likely to choose as payment? What else would he have accepted in return for the captive other than a substitute that was more exalted and great, so that, by exchanging the lesser for the greater, he might nourish more fully his own passion of pride? There is no doubt that, of all the people who existed from the beginning of time, he saw nothing in any of them to match the circumstances he saw surrounding the one who appeared at that time: conception without intercourse, a spotless birth, a virgin nursing her baby [and all the miracles and marvels recounted in the gospels]. Seeing this power, therefore, the enemy also saw in him an opportunity to receive in the exchange a greater value than that of the captive. For this reason he chooses him to be a ransom for those who are locked up in the prison of death. But it was impossible for him to look upon the unveiled vision of God, without seeing in him only a part of the flesh which he had long ago conquered through sin.

This is why the divinity was covered with flesh: so that in looking at what was well known and familiar to himself, the enemy might not be terrified at approaching the overwhelming power, and that, in perceiving the power which, although gradually, became more and more visible through the miracles, he might consider what he saw an object of desire rather than of fear. You see, then, how goodness was joined to justice, and how wisdom was not separated from them. Choosing to save is a sign of goodness; making the redemption of the captive a contractual matter displays justice; finding a device to enable the enemy to seize the incomprehensible is a sign of the highest form of wisdom. (23)

3. It is likely that a person who has paid close attention to the flow of this argument might ask where the power of the divinity and the incorruptibility of the divine power appear in what we have said. To present this clearly, let us consider the continuation of the [gospel] mystery, where power appears united intimately with love. First of all, that the all-powerful nature could even descend to the low level of humanity is a stronger proof of power than the supernatural greatness seen in the miracles. The descent to lowliness is a kind of superabundant power which cannot be limited even by things contrary to nature. The vastness of the heavens, the shining of the stars, the order of the universe, and the everlasting control over creation do not display the divine, transcendent power as much as the descent to the weakness of our nature. For in the latter case the sublime, coming into the lowly, is seen as lowly, but does not cease to be on high, and divinity, entwined with human nature, becomes the latter, but continues to be itself.

As we have already said, the nature of the hostile power could not enter into the pure presence of God or endure God's unveiled appearance; in order that the exchange for us might, therefore, be readily acceptable to the one who demanded it, the divinity was shrouded with the veil of our nature, so that, as happens with greedy fish, the hook of the divinity might be gulped down with the bait of the flesh, and, when life was brought in to dwell with death, and light shone in darkness, the exact opposites of light and life might disappear completely. (24)

Against Eunomius

4. We say that the only-begotten God brought everything into existence through himself and rules over everything by

himself; we also say that one of the things he brought into
existence was human nature, and that, when it fell into evil
and, therefore, became subject to the corruption of death, he
drew it back to eternal life through himself, assuming the
whole of the human to himself through the human person in
whom he dwelt. Thus we say that he joined his own life-
giving power to our mortal and perishable nature, and that
he transformed our state of mortality into life-giving grace
and power through union with himself. We say that this is
the mystery of the lord according to the flesh: the one who is
immutable came into being in the mutable, so that, after
transforming the evil that is mingled with our changeable
condition, and after changing it from a worse state to a
better one, he could utterly wipe it out of our nature by
destroying it himself. For "our God is a consuming fire"
(Heb. 12.29), by which every form of evil is destroyed.
(III.III.51-52)[9]

5. We reflect both upon the plan worked out through the
flesh according to its own properties and upon the divine
power in itself.[10] [Eunomius] says, as we do, that the Word
which existed in the beginning was revealed through flesh,
and yet no one ever accused him, nor did he ever accuse
himself, of preaching two Words, one who existed in the
beginning and another who became flesh; for he knows well
that the Word who appeared in flesh is the same as the Word
who was with God. But the flesh was not identical with the
divinity, until it too was transformed into the divinity, so
that some attributes could of necessity apply to the divine
Word, and others to the form of the slave.

If Eunomius, then, does not accuse himself of teaching a
duality of Words because of such a confession of faith, why
are we falsely accused of dividing the Christ of our faith into
two? We say that the one who was exceedingly exalted after

[9]Text: Jaeger, II, 125-126.

[10]The starting-point for the entire discussion of which this selection is the
conclusion is the following text: "Let all the house of Israel, therefore, know with
certainty that God has made him lord and Christ, this Jesus whom you crucified"
(Acts 2.36).

suffering became lord and Christ because of his union with the true lord and Christ. We know from what we have learned that the divine nature is always one and the same, and that it exists in the same way.

The flesh, on the other hand, is in itself whatever reason and sensation discover about it; when united to the divine, however, it no longer exists with its own limitations and characteristics, but is assumed into the superior, transcendent reality. But the contemplation of the respective characteristics of the flesh and the divinity keeps them clear and distinct, as long as each of them is looked at in itself. Say, for example, that the Word existed before the ages, but the flesh came into being in the last times; one may not reverse this and say that the flesh existed before time and the Word came into being in the last times. The flesh has a passive nature, and the Word an active one, so that the flesh does not create other beings, nor does the divinity have the ability to suffer; the Word was in the beginning with God (see Jn. 1.1), while the human being was subject to testing by death; the human was not eternal, nor was the divine mortal. And everything else is viewed in the same way.

The human nature did not give life to Lazarus, nor was it the power that could not suffer which wept for him as he lay dead; the tear belongs to the human, and life to true life (see Jn. 11.35-44). Human poverty does not feed the multitudes, and the almighty power does not run to the fig tree (see Mt. 21.19). Who is weary from the journey (see Jn. 4.6), and who, by a word, tirelessly gives the whole universe existence? What is the radiance of the glory (see Heb. 1.3), and what was pierced by nails (see Jn. 20.25)? Which form is beaten in the passion (see Mt. 26.67), and which is eternally glorified? This much is clear: the blows belong to the servant in whom the master is, while the honors belong to the master whom the servant encloses; because of their joining and unity, therefore, each of them shares the characteristics of the other—the master takes the servant's bruises on himself, and the servant is glorified by the master's honor. That is why one speaks of the cross of "the lord of glory" (I Cor. 2.8), and why "every tongue confesses that Jesus Christ is lord, to the glory of God the Father" (Phil. 2.11).

Let us now reflect upon what dies and what destroys death, upon what is renewed and what is emptied. The divinity is emptied (see Phil. 2.6), so that it could be accessible to the human nature; the human is renewed and becomes divine through its union with the divine. When the true life which was in the flesh rushed back to itself after the suffering, the flesh that surrounded it was raised with it, and was pushed up from corruption to incorruptibility by divine immortality.

Consider fire, which is often hidden from view in wood and escapes the notice of those who see or even touch it, although it is seen clearly when it flares up; this is how he acted in death, who by his own power separated the soul from the body; he said to his own father, "Into your hands I entrust my spirit" (Lk. 23.46), just as he said, "having the power to put it [i.e., my life] down, and having the power to take it again" (Jn. 10.18). He despised what was shameful among human beings because he was the lord of glory, concealed, as it were, the embers of life in his bodily nature, and, through the divine plan based on his death, revived and rekindled those embers through the power of his own divinity. In this way he gave the warmth of life back to that which had died and saturated that humble first-fruit of our nature with the infinity of the divine power.

In this way he changed that first-fruit into what he was. He changed the form of a servant into lord, and changed the human born of Mary into Christ; he changed the one who was crucified out of weakness into life and power, and he caused everything that was piously seen in the divine Word to be also in the one assumed by the Word. As a result, these qualities do not seem to be in each one independently, according to some type of division; instead, the perishable nature, through its union with the divine, has been remade in accordance with the superior part and participates in the power of the divinity. It is just as if someone said that mixing a drop of vinegar in the sea turned it into sea-water, because this liquid's natural quality no longer existed due to the infinity of the greater part.

What we say proclaims, not a plurality of Christs, as Eunomius charges, but rather a union of the human person with the divine, and it labels "transformation" the process by which the mortal becomes immortal, the servant becomes lord, sin becomes justification, curse becomes blessing, and the human becomes Christ. How else can the slanderers, then, prove that we preach two Christs in our doctrine, simply because we deny that the lord, Christ, Word, and God, who existed in an uncreated fashion from the beginning out of the Father, was made? We declare that the blessed Peter was referring briefly and incidentally to the mystery concerning the flesh, in accordance with the meaning we have explained: what was crucified because of weakness has itself, through the overwhelming power of the one dwelling in it, become exactly what the indweller is and is called, and, as we said, is therefore called lord and Christ. (III.III.62-69)[11]

6. Although Paul proclaims the union of the human with the divine everywhere, he nonetheless recognizes in each one its own qualities; and so human weakness is changed for the better through its participation in the perfect, while the divine power is not debased because of its joining with the lowly nature. When he says, therefore, that "he did not spare his own son" (Rom. 8.32), he is distinguishing the true son from other sons, who were born, exalted, and rejected (I am referring to those who were brought into existence at his command), and he points to the relationship according to nature by adding the word "own." To avoid anybody's attributing the suffering on the cross to the perfect nature, he rectifies this terrible aberration clearly by the use of other words, and calls him "mediator between God and humans," "human being," and "God" (I Tim. 2.5), so that, by stating these two points about the one reality, the appropriate quality might be contemplated in each: the inability to suffer for

[11]Text: Jaeger, II, 129-133.

the divine, and the divine plan based on suffering for the human.

Since Paul's thought, therefore, divides that which was united out of love for humanity (although distinguished in word), when he proclaims the reality that is superior to, and surpasses all understanding, he employs more exalted terms and calls him God over all, mighty God, power of God, wisdom (see I Cor. 1.24), and so on. When, however, he alludes to all the suffering necessarily experienced because of the assumption of our weakness, he names the combination from our side and calls him a human being; he does not bring that which is designated by this word down to the level of the rest of this nature, but uses it so that reverence toward both may be preserved. The human is glorified through its assumption, and the divine is not defiled by its descent, but hands the human part over to suffering, while effecting, through the divine power, the resurrection of that which suffered. In this way the experience of death is not attributed to the one who participated in the nature that could suffer because the human was united to him; at the same time, the exalted names that apply to God come down upon the human, so that the one who appeared on the cross is called "lord of glory" (see I Cor. 2.8), because the favor of these names is transferred from the divine to the human through the unity of his nature with the lowly one. (III.IV.13-16)[12]

7. Remaining what he was, namely, God, Word, life, light, grace, truth, lord, Christ, and every exalted, divine title, he became, in the assumed human being who was none of these, everything else that the Word was; and along with all that he became Christ and lord, as Peter teaches and Eunomius confesses, but not through the divinity's assuming something that would perfect it, for all exalted glory is seen in the divine nature. And so he became both Christ and lord, not by achieving the addition of grace to the divinity, for it is agreed that the nature of the divinity possesses all good, but by leading the human to that form of participation in the

[12]Text: Jaeger, II, 138-140.

divinity which is signified by the titles Christ and lord. (III.IV.22)[13]

8. The only-begotten God, who is in the bosom of the Father (see Jn. 1.18), is Word, king, lord, and everything exalted in name and thought, and therefore does not need to become anything good, since he is himself the fullness of all good things; he changes into something and becomes what he was not before. Just as the one who did not know sin became sin (see II Cor. 5.21), to take away the sin of the world, in the same way the flesh which received the lord became lord and Christ; it was not such by nature, but was transformed into this through the union. From this we learn that God would not have appeared in the flesh (see I Tim. 3.16), if the Word had not become flesh (see Jn. 1.14), nor would the flesh of the human person that covered the Word have been transformed into the divine, if that which appeared had not become Christ and lord. (III.IV.45-46)[14]

C. GREGORY OF NAZIANZUS

Letter 101 (To Cledonius)[15]

1. Let these people [the heretics] stop deceiving themselves and others by maintaining that what they call the lord's human person, who is rather our lord and God, lacks a human mind. We do not separate the human person from the divinity, for we teach and confess one and the same individual, who was at first not a human person, but God and only Son, existing before time, without any body or bodily elements. This person is in the end a human person as well, a reality which was assumed for our salvation, and which can suffer because of its flesh, but is also immune to suffering due to its divinity; it is limited by its body, but unlimited since it is spirit; this same one is both earthly and

---

[13]Text: Jaeger, II, 142.

[14]Text: Jaeger, II, 151-152.

[15]Text: SC, 208, 40-60.

heavenly, visible and yet an object of thought, comprehensible and incomprehensible—all this so that the whole human person, which had fallen through sin, might be created anew through the power of one and the same person who is both totally human and God. (12-15)

2. Whoever does not believe that Mary is mother of God is cut off from the divinity. Separated from God in the same way is anyone who says that he passed through the virgin as though through a channel, without being formed in her in a way that was both divine, since there was no man involved, and human, because of the normal process of pregnancy. Anyone who says that the human person was formed first and that God then slipped into him should be condemned. For this is not a begetting of God, but a means of avoiding begetting. Anyone who introduces two sons, one the Son of the God who is Father, and a second one born of the mother, loses the adoption promised to those who have true faith (see Rom. 8.5 and 23). For there are two natures, God and the human person, since a soul and a body are here; but there are not two sons or two gods. And there are not two human persons, even if Paul did speak in this way about the interior human person and the exterior one (see II Cor. 4.16 and Eph. 3.16). (16-19)

3. To put it briefly, if the invisible is not the same as the visible, and if the timeless is not the same as that which is subject to time, then the savior is composed of two different elements, but not of two different persons. What a terrible idea that is! For the two are one by their union: God on the one hand became human, while the human became god—or however one should best express this. I say two different elements, contrary to what happens in the trinity; for there it is a question of one person and another, so that we do not mix together the individual existents. There it is not one element and another, since the three are one and the same because of the divinity. (20-21)

4. Anyone who says that the divinity worked in him through grace, as in a prophet, but was not, and is not joined to him in substance, would be empty of the higher power, or

rather full of its opposite. Whoever does not worship the crucified one is accursed and to be numbered among the murderers of God. Accursed too is anyone who says that he was made perfect by his actions, so that, either after his baptism or after his resurrection from the dead, he was judged worthy of adoptive sonship, in the way that the Greeks introduce people whom they enrolled among the gods. For anything that begins, progresses, or is made perfect is not God, even if such statements are made because of an ongoing revelation (see Lk. 2.52). (22-24)

5. Anyone who says that his flesh has been put aside and that the divinity has been stripped from the body, so that he does not now exist and will not return with that which was assumed, should not see the glory of his coming. For where is the body now, if it is not with the one who assumed it? It has not been stored away in the sun, as the Manichaeans insanely say, in order to honor it by dishonor. Nor did it dissipate or dissolve into thin air, as happens, by their very nature, to sounds, to the aroma of perfume, and to a bolt of lightning which passes by and does not stop. How can we explain his having been touched after the resurrection (see Lk. 24.39 and Jn. 20.27), and his even being seen afterwards by those who had pierced him? For the divinity is by nature invisible. In my opinion he will come with the body, in the same way that he was seen by, or appeared to the disciples on the mountain, when the divinity overwhelmed the weak flesh (see Mt. 17.2). And just as we make these latter statements to get rid of suspicion, so we make the former ones to correct any false innovations. (25-29)

6. Anyone who says that the flesh descended from heaven, and is not from this earth and from us should be condemned. For it is because of union with the one from heaven that statements like the following are made: "The second human from heaven" (I Cor. 15.47); "as the heavenly one, so too the heavenly beings" (I Cor. 15.48); "No one has gone up into heaven, except for the one who came down from heaven, the Son of man" (Jn. 3.13). The words "all things were made through Christ" (see Jn. 1.3) and "Christ dwells

in our hearts" (Eph. 3.17) are said, not because God is visible, but because God can be known by our minds; and so, just as the natures are intermingled, so too the names are intertwined with each other by reason of their being joined. (30-31)

7. Those who have placed their hopes in a human being without reason are truly irrational themselves and absolutely unworthy of salvation. For what was not assumed was not cured. But whatever has been united to God is saved. If half of Adam fell, then it was half that was assumed and saved. But if the whole Adam fell, then that was joined to the whole begotten one and was saved as a whole. Let them not begrudge us total salvation, therefore, and let them not invest the savior only with bones, sinews, and the mere image of a human being. If the human does not have a soul, that is what the Arians say in order to attribute the passion to the divinity, since what moves the body is also what suffers. But if it has a soul and yet lacks reason, then how can it be human? For the human being is not an irrational animal. In this case the appearance and the dwelling place would have to be human, while the soul would have to be that of a horse, an ox, or some other irrational animal. This, then, is what will be saved, and I shall have been deceived by truth, since one reality will have been honored with salvation, while another boasts of that honor. But if the human is intelligent and not mindless, let them stop being so totally mindless themselves. (32-35)

"But," someone will say, "the divinity was powerful enough to replace the mind." What, then, does this mean for me? Divinity with flesh alone is not human, just as divinity with a soul alone is not human; and neither is divinity with both of these, but without a mind, which is the factor that particularly constitutes a human being. Preserve the human part complete, therefore, and mix in the divinity, so that you might do good for me in a perfect way. "But," the argument goes on, "he did not consist of two complete realities." No indeed, if you consider the matter from the material viewpoint. For a fifteen gallon jug will not hold thirty gallons, nor will one body's space hold two or more bodies. But if you look at spiritual and non-bodily reality, consider that I myself consist of a soul, a reason, a mind, and a holy spirit, and that before me, this universe, I mean the totality of things seen and unseen, encompassed the Father, the Son, and the Holy spirit (see Col. 1.16). For the nature of spiritual realities is such that they can be mingled with one another and with bodies in a non-bodily way and without being cut up. (36-39)

9. "But," one might say, "our mind has been condemned." What about the flesh? Has it not been condemned? Either reject the flesh because of sin, or bring in the mind because of salvation. If the lesser reality was assumed, so that it could be sanctified through his becoming flesh, will not the greater reality also be assumed, so that it might be sanctified through his becoming human? If the clay was leavened and became a "new dough" (I Cor. 5.7), will not the image also be leavened and mixed together with God, having been made divine by the divinity? We shall add another point: if the mind is totally rejected, on the grounds that it is sinful and has been condemned, so that the body was therefore assumed, while the mind was ignored, then people who sin through the mind have a perfect excuse for their actions, since, in that case, God's testimony would have shown clearly that the mind cannot be healed. (46-47)

10. Shall I state a more important point? In speaking like this, you dishonor my mind, in order to bind God to the flesh, as though God could be bound in no other way, and for this reason you tear down the partition between them; if I worship a human being, you worship flesh. My opinion, although I am neither a scientist nor a scholar, is that mind is mingled with mind, since it is closer to it and more like it; and, through it, mind is mingled with flesh, since mind acts as a mediator between divinity and the grossness of flesh. (48-49)

11. Let us see next how they explain the reason for his becoming human, or, as they say, becoming flesh. If the point was that God, who is otherwise infinite, might be

placed within limits and could thus converse with human beings in the flesh as through a veil, then their dramatic mask and the play they act out is clever indeed; but I will not mention the fact that God could have conversed with us in other ways, as in a burning bush (see Ex. 3.2), and, as even earlier, in human form (see Gen. 18.1). But if the point was to wipe out the condemnation of sin, sanctifying like by like, then, just as he needed flesh because of the condemned flesh, and soul for the soul, so too he needed a mind for the sake of the mind, which not only fell in Adam, but was the first to be ill, as doctors say about illnesses. (50-51)

12. If they take refuge in the claim that God could have saved the human without a mind, then it would also have been possible to do this without flesh, by a sheer act of will, in the same way that God, without a body, does, and has done all other things. (54)

Oration 7 (Panegyric for His Brother Caesarius)[16]

13. I am small and great, humble and lofty, mortal and immortal, earthly and heavenly. I share the one set of qualities with the lower world, and the other one with God; one set belongs to the flesh, and the other belongs to the spirit. I must be buried with Christ, rise up with Christ, share Christ's inheritance, become a child of God, and even become God. See where the progress of our discourse has led us. I can almost give thanks for the suffering which has caused me to reflect in this way, and because of which I have come to long for departure from this life. This is the meaning of the great mystery for us. This is God's plan for us; for our sake God became human and poor, to raise up the flesh, to restore the image, to form the human anew, in order that we might all become one in Christ, who became perfectly, in all of us, everything that he is in himself, so that we might no longer be male and female, barbarian, Scythian, slave, or free (all of which are characteristics of the flesh), but might

16Text: PG, 35.785.

carry in ourselves only the divine image, through which and in which we were made, and according to which we were so formed and molded, that we can be recognized through it alone. (23)

Oration 8 (Funeral Oration for His Sister Gorgonia)[17]

14. O nature of woman, which proved superior to that of man because of the common struggle for salvation, and which proved that male and female differ in body, not in soul. (14)

Oration 29 (Third Theological Oration)[18]

15. To put it briefly, attribute the more lofty qualities to the divinity, the nature which is superior to suffering and the body; attribute the more humble qualities to the composite, the one who for you was emptied and became flesh (see Phil. 2.7 and Jn. 1.14), or, since it is no shame to say it, became human, and was then exalted (see Phil. 2.9), so that you could get rid of all that is fleshly and earthly in your beliefs, and learn how to be more lofty and how to rise up to the divinity, and that in addition you might not rest in visible reality, but could be raised up to the spiritual world and understand which words deal with the [divine] nature and which treat of the divine plan. (18)

16. For the one whom you now despise had a prior existence higher than you; the one who is now human was once not a composite being. He remained what he was, and assumed what he was not. He existed in the beginning without a cause; for what is a cause of God? But later on he came into being for a cause, namely, to save the insolent one, you, who despise the divinity, because it assumed your earthly grossness. He came together with flesh through the mediatorship of mind; the human here below became God, since it was mingled with, and became one with God because it was

[17]Text: PG, 35.805.
[18]Text: SC, 250, 216-218.

conquered by the greater part—this was done so that I could become God to the extent that God became human. He was born, but he had also been begotten; he was born of woman, but of one who was also a virgin. The first shows humanity, the second divinity. He had no father on the human side, and no mother on the divine. All this points to divinity. (19)

Oration 30 (Fourth Theological Oration)

17. He was truly a slave to flesh, birth, and our human sufferings, for the sake of our freedom and for all those who were captives of sin and whom he saved. What greater thing can happen to human lowliness than to be entwined with God, to become God through this mingling, and to be "visited from on high by the dawn" (Lk. 1.78), in such a way that "the holy one that was born was called Son of the most high" (Lk. 1.32), and was given "the name which is above every name" (Lk. 1.32)? And what other name is this but God? (3)[19]

18. He was not forsaken by the Father or, as some people think, by his own divinity, as though it were afraid of suffering and for that reason withdrew from him in his suffering. For who forced him to be born down here or to go up on the cross in the first place? He represents us, as I have said, in himself. For we were formerly abandoned and despised, but have now been taken up and saved through the suffering of the one who could not suffer. (5)[20]

19. In the "form of a servant" (Phil. 2.7) he comes down to those who are his fellow servants and his servants, and he takes on a totally different form; he bears in himself all of me, along with all that is mine, so that in himself he might destroy evil, as fire does wax, or as the sun does the mist of the earth, and so that, through this mingling, I might share in what is his. (6)[21]

---

[19]Text: SC, 250, 230.
[20]Text: SC, 250, 234.
[21]Text: SC, 250, 236.

20. To intercede does not mean, as it does for most human beings, to seek vengeance, since that would flow from a certain lowly quality; it means, rather, acting on our behalf by virtue of his mediatorship, just as the Spirit is also said to intercede for us (see Rom. 8.26). "For there is one God, and one mediator between God and humans, the human Jesus Christ" (I Tim. 2.5). And, since he is with the body that he assumed, he continues to intercede even now, as a human being, for my salvation, until he makes me God through the power of his having become human, even though he is no longer known according to the flesh, that is to say, with fleshly passions and all that is ours, except for sin (see Heb. 4.15). And so "we have Jesus for our advocate" (I Jn. 2.1), not as one who prostrates himself before the Father for us and falls down like a slave. Forget this idea, which in itself is slave-like and unworthy of the Spirit. It is not in the Father's nature to demand this, nor is it in the Son's nature to submit to it. Is it proper even to think this of God? As Word and counsellor, he persuades God, through his sufferings as a human being, to be patient. This is what advocacy means to me. (14)[22]

21. He is called light (see Jn. 8.12 and 9.5), since he is the brilliance of souls that were cleansed in their word and in their life. For if ignorance and sin are darkness, then knowledge and life filled with God are light. He is called life (see Jn. 14.6), because he is light and gives form and independent existence to every rational nature. He is called redemption (see I Cor. 1.30), because he frees us from the slavery of sin and gives himself for us as a ransom which purifies the world. He is called resurrection (see Jn. 11.25), because he raises us up from here and leads us back to life, although we were dead from having tasted [sin]. (20)[23]

22. The titles [described in the preceding selection] are common to the one who exists above us and the one who exists on our behalf. The following ones belong properly to

[22]Text: SC, 250, 256.
[23]Text: SC, 250, 268-270.

us and to what he assumed from us: he is a human being (see Jn. 9.11), not only to be able to approach bodies with a body, because otherwise he could not have approached them, since his nature was incomprehensible; no, he is human, so as to be able to sanctify the human through himself, becoming like leaven for the whole dough (see I Cor. 5.6). He united to himself that which had been condemned, so that he could free all of it from condemnation, and he became for all of us everything that we were (except for sin), i.e., body, soul, and mind, through which death came; he is the composite of all these, a human being, God in visible form, because he still is spiritual. He is called "son of man" (Mt. 9.6), because of Adam and the virgin, from both of whom he was born—from him as from a forefather, and from her as from a true mother, although not in the usual way of procreation. He is Christ because of his divinity; for this is an anointing of the humanity, and it sanctifies, not by action, as in the case of other christs, but by the total presence of the one who does the anointing. The effect of this presence is to call the anointing party a human being and to make the one anointed God. (21)[24]

Oration 37[25]

23. It seems to me that this question which you have asked touches on the respect which is shown to chastity, and that it demands a kind response. I see that the majority of people are badly disposed toward chastity, and that their laws concerning it are unequal and unfair. For why else would they have restrained the female, while indulging the male? A woman who has deliberately sinned against her husband's bed is guilty of adultery and is subject to the harsh legal penalties attached to that sin. But a man who does the same thing to his wife is judged guilty only of fornication and goes unpunished. I do not accept this legislation and I do not approve this custom. The legislators were males, and that is

[24]Text: SC, 250, 270-272.
[25]Text: SC, 318, 282-286.

why the legislation is anti-female. They entrusted children to their father's authority, but left the weaker part uncared for.

God does not act like this. God says, "Honor your father and your mother, so that it might go well for you; this is the first commandment with a promise" (see Ex. 20.12 and Eph. 6.2). God also says, "Let whoever curses father or mother die by the death" (Ex. 21.17). At one and the same time God honored good and punished evil. Scripture also says, "A father's blessing props up the children's homes, while a mother's curse uproots the foundations" (Sir. 3.11 [LXX, 3.9]). Look at the equality of this legislation: one creator of man and woman, one dust for both, one image, one law, one death, one resurrection; we are born equally from a man and from a woman, and children owe one duty to both their parents. (6)

24. How, then, can you ask for chastity, but not give it in return? How can you demand what you do not give? How can you pass unfair legislation, when your bodies deserve equal honor? Look at the lower realities of life; The woman sinned; so did Adam. The serpent deceived both of them; one was not found weaker and the other stronger. Or look at higher reality: Christ saves both through his sufferings. Did he become flesh for the man? He did it for the woman as well. Did he die for the man? The woman too is saved through his death. He is said to be "from the seed of David" (Rom. 1.3); perhaps you think that this favors the man. But he is also born of a virgin, and this is a plus for the woman. (7)

Oration 45

25. The Word of God—existing before time, invisible, incomprehensible, bodiless, beginning from beginning, light from light, source of life and of immortality, expression of the archetype, the unmoved seal, the unchangeable image, the definition and Word of the Father—comes to its own image, wears flesh for the sake of flesh, is joined to an intellectual soul for the sake of my soul (cleansing like by like), and becomes human in all respects, except for sin (see Heb.

4.15). He was conceived by the virgin, after she had been purified in soul and flesh by the Spirit. He came forth as God, along with that which he had assumed—one reality from two opposite ones, flesh and spirit; one of these conferred divinity, while the other received it. What a marvelous new mixture this is! The one who is comes into being, and the uncreated is created; the one who has no limitations is limited by the intervention of an intellectual soul mediating between the divinity and the grossness of the flesh. The one who enriches others is poor, for he takes on my poor flesh, so that I might be rich with his divinity. The one who is full is emptied, for he is emptied of his own glory for a while, so that I might share in his fullness.

What are the riches of this goodness? What is the mystery that surrounds me? I shared in the image, but did not preserve it; he shares in my flesh, in order to save the image and make the flesh immortal. He communicates a second sharing that is much more wonderful than the first, for at that time he gave a share in the greater, while now he takes a share in the inferior. (9)[26]

26. To whom was it shed on our behalf, and why—the blood, mighty and famous, of God, the high priest and offering? We were held in captivity by the evil one, when we were sold into the control of sin and received pleasure in exchange for wickedness. But if the ransom belongs to no one else than the one who holds the captive, then I ask, to whom was it paid, and why? If it was paid to the evil one, then it is a shocking outrage, when the thief not only is paid a ransom by God, but actually receives God as a ransom for his tyranny and as a superlative reward, because of which he should, in all justice, have spared us. But if it was paid to the Father, then first of all I ask how this could be, since we were not under his control. Secondly, for what reason did the blood of the only begotten one delight a Father who did not accept Isaac when he was offered by his father, but changed the sacrificial offering, replacing the human being with a ram?

[26]Text: PG, 36.633-635.

It is clear, is it not, that the Father takes this offering, not because he demanded or needed it, but because of the eternal plan, and because the human had to be sanctified through the humanity of God, so that he could free us by forcefully conquering the tyrant, and could lead us to himself through the mediation of the Son, who carried out this plan for the glory of the Father, whom he clearly obeys in all things? (22)[27]

3. JOHN CHRYSOSTOM

Homily X on the Gospel of John[28]

1. "He came to his own, and his own people did not receive him" (Jn. 1.11).

Since God loves human beings and is beneficent, God takes pains to do everything so that we can radiate virtue. God wants us to win glory, and to this end draws no one by force or constraint; instead God attracts, by persuasion and kindness, all those who are willing to respond, and thus wins them over. Some, therefore, received him when he came, while others did not. For God wishes to have no servant who is unwilling or who was forced into service; God wants all to come of their own free will and choice, and with gratitude to God for this grace. Human beings keep servants against their will through the law of ownership, since they need the services of such people. But God lacks nothing, has no need for anything of ours, and does everything for the sake of our salvation alone, putting us in control of this matter; that is why God uses no force or constraint on anyone who is unwilling. God looks only to what is good for us, and being dragged to this service against one's will is the equivalent of not serving at all.

2. "Why then," someone will say, "does God punish those who are unwilling to obey? Why did God threaten Gehenna

[27]Text: PG, 36.653.

[28]Text: PG, 59.73-78.

for those who do not listen to God's commands?" The reason is that God, who is very good, cares deeply for us even when we do not obey, and does not abandon us even when we turn away and flee from God. Since we rejected God's first approach through kindness and were unwilling to go on the road of persuasion and beneficence, God paved a second way, based on punishment and retribution; this is a way that is indeed bitter, but nonetheless necessary. For when the first pathway was scorned, it became necessary to develop a second one.

3. Lawmakers inflict many harsh punishments on people who break the law, and we do not reject them for this, but honor them all the more because of these punishments. They need nothing from us and often do not even know who is going to enjoy the help of the laws they have passed; still they kept the good order of our lives in mind and honored those who live virtuously, while restraining through punishment the licentious and those who would disturb other people's peace. If we marvel at these people and feel affection for them, should we not be more deeply in awe of, and in love with, God because of God's great care for us? There is an infinite difference between God's providence for us and their concern. For the richness of God's goodness is inexpressible and surpasses all limits (see Rom. 2.4 and Eph. 2.7).

4. Consider this: "He came to his own"—not for his own sake (for God, as I have said, needs nothing), but for the good of his own. "And his own people did not receive him," even though he came to his own for their good; instead they rejected him, and not only that, but they threw him out of the vineyard and killed him (see Mt. 21.39). But still he did not bar them from repentance; even after such transgressions, if they would will it, he made it possible, through faith in him, for all their sins to be washed away and for them to be made equal to those who had done nothing like this and were his closest friends.

5. Everything found in the words of blessed Paul testify clearly that I am not simply making this up to produce a persuasive argument. After the crucifixion Paul persecuted

Christ and stoned Christ's martyr, Stephen, through the many hands that he helped; but when he repented, condemned the sins he had committed, and ran to the one he had persecuted, Christ numbered him among his friends immediately and put him among the leaders, by declaring him—"the blasphemer, persecutor, and insulter" (I Tim. 1.13)—a herald and teacher of the whole world. In his joy at God's love of humanity, Paul made this proclamation without shame; he recorded his past sins in his writings, as on a pillar, and declared them to all, for he thought that exposing his past life to public view in order to proclaim the greatness of God's gift was better than hiding God's unspeakable and inexpressible love for humanity out of a reluctance to reveal his own sinfulness. He, therefore, talks constantly of the persecution, the plots, the battles against the church, saying, for example, "I am not worthy to be called an apostle, for I persecuted the church of God" (I Cor. 15.9); he also says that "Jesus came to save sinners, of whom I am the chief" (I Tim. 1.15), and, "You have heard of my way of life when I was a Jew: that I persecuted the church of God terribly and tried to destroy it" (Gal. 1.13). (1)

6. Thus Paul makes a kind of return to Christ for Christ's patience with him, by showing who and what a hostile enemy it was that Christ saved. In the same way he quite openly preaches about the battle which he zealously waged against Christ in the beginning, and then holds out good hope for those who had fallen into despair. For he says that Christ accepted him for this reason, that in him first of all Christ might "display great patience" and the overwhelming richness of his goodness, "as a model for those who were going to believe in him for eternal life" (I Tim. 1.16). For what they had done was beyond the possibility of pardon, as the evangelist declared when he said, "He came to his own, and his own people did not receive him" (Jn. 1.11)

7. Where did he come from, the one who fills all things and is present everywhere? What place did he empty of his presence, the one who holds all things in his hand and controls them? He did not change places; how could that be? He

did this by coming down to our level. For although he was in the world, he did not seem to be there, since he was not yet known; but since he showed himself later on by deigning to assume our flesh, John calls this manifestation and descent a coming. It is amazing that the disciple feels no shame at the master's dishonor, and even records openly the insult directed at the master; and this is no small sign of the way in which he loves the truth. In any case, one who feels shame should be ashamed of those who offer an insult, not of the one who has been treated with contempt. For he appeared all the more glorious here, in that, even after being insulted, he showed great concern for those who had offered the insult; and they in turn were seen by all to be ungrateful and defiled, because they rejected as a hateful enemy the one who came to them with such good things. They were injured, not only in this way, but also because they did not obtain what those who received him obtained. And what did they obtain?

8. "As many as received him, to them he gave power to be children of God" (Jn. 1.12), says the evangelist.

Why then, blessed one, do you not tell us about the punishment of those who did not receive him, instead of saying that they were his own, and when he came to his own, they did not receive him? Why did you not tell us as well what they will suffer for this, and what punishment they will undergo? By doing this you would have struck great fear into them, and your threats would have softened their stubborn insanity. Why, then, did you keep silent? He replies, "What punishment can be greater than this—to have the power to become children of God, and not to become such, but to deprive oneself voluntarily of this type of excellence and honor?" Their punishment will not only consist in their not receiving anything good; the everlasting fire will welcome them as well, as he revealed more clearly in what he said later on. In the meantime, he talks about the ineffable goods of those who received him, and he sums them up briefly in these words, when he says, "Whoever received him, to them he gave power to become children of God." "All people," he says, "have been judged worthy of this honor, whether they are slave or free, Greek, barbarian, or Scythian, foolish or wise, female or male, young or old, common or noble, rich or poor, ruler or private citizen." For faith and the grace of the Spirit have removed the inequality caused by worldly values, have molded all into one form, and have sealed them with one image—the royal one.

9. What else could equal a love for humanity like this? A king, who is formed of the same clay as we are, does not deign to enroll in the royal army his fellow servants who have the same nature as he, but are often better in character than he, simply because they happen to be servants. But the only one begotten of God did not refuse to number among the ranks of God's children tax-collectors, sorcerers, slaves, and the most dishonored of all, people with bodies that were mutilated and horribly maimed. Such is the great power of faith in him; such is the overwhelming force of grace. When the substance of fire comes together with earth from the mines, it immediately makes gold out of the earth; in the same way, and much more so, does baptism change those who are washed from clay into gold, when the Spirit, like fire, falls into our souls at that time, burning up "the image of the earthly one," and bringing forth "the image of the heavenly one" (I Cor. 15.49), newly minted and shining, and gleaming as though just out of the smelting furnace.

10. Why did he not say that he made them children of God, instead of "He gave them power to become children of God"? He did this to show that one needs great zeal to be able to preserve pure and undefiled forever the image of adoption stamped in us at baptism; he also shows that no one can take this power away from us, if we do not choose to deprive ourselves of it first. People who have received absolute authority over certain matters in human affairs have almost as much power as those who gave them the authority; how much more powerful than all others will we be, who have received this honor from God, if we avoid doing anything unworthy of this power, simply because the one who gave us this honor is better and greater than all? At the same time he also wants to show that grace does not simply

appear on the scene, but comes only to those who are willing and eager; for becoming children lies in the power of those people, since, if they do not make the choice first, then the gift does not come upon them nor does it have any effect. (2)

Homily XI on the Gospel of John[29]

11. "And the Word was made flesh," he says, "and dwelt among us" (Jn. 1.14)

After saying that those who received him were born of God and became children of God, he states the basic cause underlying this ineffable honor, which is the fact that the Word became flesh, and the lord assumed the form of the slave (see Phil. 2.7). The one who is a natural Son of God became a son of man, in order to make children of God out of the sons of men. The lofty is mingled with the lowly, but suffers no damage to its own glory, while the lowly rises out of the depths of its lowliness. This is what happened with Christ. He in no way diminished his own nature through this descent, but raised us, who were sitting forever in dishonor and darkness, up to indescribable glory. In somewhat the same way a king, who speaks with care and concern to a very poor person, in no way shames himself, but makes the poor person illustrious and admired by all. In a case of transitory human glory, therefore, association with an inferior does no damage to a superior; how much truer is this, then, when it is a question of that pure and blessed essence which has nothing transitory about it (either by means of loss or gain), but possesses all good things unchangeably and in a fixed form forever? So when you hear that "The Word became flesh," do not be upset or disturbed. The [divine] essence did not change into flesh (it is sacrilegious even to think this); it remained what it was and assumed the form of the servant. (1)

12. Why, then, did he use the word "became"? He used it to shut the mouths of heretics. Since there are some who say that the whole of God's plan of salvation was an illusion, a

[29]Text: PG, 59.77-80.

sham, and an empty show, he added the word "became" to do away with their blasphemy right form the start; he wanted to proclaim, therefore, not a change of substance (God forbid!), but rather the assumption of real flesh. It is the same as when [Paul] says, "Christ redeemed us from the curse of the law, becoming a curse for us" (Gal. 3.13); he does not mean by this that his substance withdrew from its own glory and changed into the substance of a curse—this thought would not even occur to the demons, or to people who are quite mad or who have lost their natural senses; it is completely insane as well as blasphemous—he does not mean this, therefore, but rather that he assumed the curse pronounced against us, and does not allow us to be under the curse any longer. In the same way here, he means that the Word became flesh, not by changing its substance into flesh, but by having assumed flesh, while that [divine] substance remains untouched.

13. But if they should say that, as God, he can do all things, so that he could even change into flesh, we would answer them by saying that he can indeed do all things, as long as he continues to be God. But if he underwent a change, and that a change for the worse, how could he be God? For change is foreign to that nature which contains no parts. That is why the prophet said, "All will grow old like a cloak, and you will roll them up like a garment, and they will be changed. But you are the same, and your years will not end" (Ps. 102.26-27). This essence is above all change. Nor is there anything greater than God, so that God could attain to it by making progress. And why do I talk about greater? There is nothing equal to God, and nothing even close to that. The only possibility, therefore, is that God changed for the worse, if indeed God did change; but this would not be God. Let the blasphemy fall, however, on the heads of those who say such things.

14. To understand that the word "became" was used only to keep you from suspecting an illusion, consider how the evangelist clarifies the discussion and does away with this evil suspicion through what follows; for he added, "And

dwelt among us." With this he all but says, "Do not suspect anything unusual because of the word 'became'. For I did not mean a change in that unchanging nature, but rather an indwelling or inhabiting." That which dwells cannot be the same as the place where it dwells, but must be something different. For one thing dwells in another; otherwise it would not be a case of dwelling, since nothing dwells in itself. When I said different, I meant according to substance; for the divine Word and the flesh are one by a union and a joining, not through a mixture or obliteration of the substances, but through a certain ineffable and awesome union. Do not ask how this took place; the Word knows what "became" means.

15. What, then, is the dwelling place which the Word inhabited? Listen to the prophet who says, "I will raise up the dwelling place of David which had fallen" (Amos 9.11). Our nature had truly fallen, and had fallen with an incurable fall, and it needed only that powerful hand. For the only way to raise it up was for the one who had shaped it in the beginning to stretch out a hand to it and shape it perfectly all over again through the rebirth of water and the Spirit. And here is the awesome and hidden mystery: the Word inhabits the dwelling forever; for it put on our flesh, never to lay it down again, but to have it with it forever. If this were not so, the Word would not have judged it worthy of the royal throne, nor would the Word, while wearing it, have been worshipped by the whole army above—angels, archangels, thrones, principalities, dominions, and powers. What word, what idea can express this great honor, so truly marvellous and awe-inspiring, that was bestowed on our human race? What angel or archangel could express it? No one anywhere, in heaven or on earth, could do it. For God's works are so great, and God's kindnesses are so mighty and marvellous, that an accurate description of them is beyond not only the human tongue, but even an angel's power.

16. We too, therefore, shall stop talking for a while and be silent; all we recommend to you is this: repay this great benefactor of ours with a payment that will in turn bring great profit back to us. This payment consists in our show-

ing careful concern for our souls. For this too is a mark of God's love for humanity, that the one who needs nothing from us says that it is ample repayment if we take care of our souls. It is, therefore, an act of sheer madness, and one deserving dreadful punishment, not to contribute what we can, after we have been given such great honor; this is especially so, since the profit from all this comes back to us again, and since innumerable good things are available to us in them. For all of this let us give thanks to the God who loves humanity, not only through our words, but much more through our actions, so that we might obtain the good of the future life. (2)

Chapter Five

Later Latin Writers

I. Introduction

The Latin writers presented here lived in the fourth and fifth centuries and were bishops of the cities attached to their names. The Western church was not embroiled in the theological controversies that raged in the East, for its teachers seemed generally content to accept the tradition they received as clearly defined truth and to hand it on quietly, without a great deal of discussion or argumentation. Their conceptual framework and terminology are often derived from Tertullian, and they offer a variety of theories as to the way in which salvation was effected. What these writers have to say on Christ and salvation will, therefore, add little that is new to what has already been seen, but they will deepen one's understanding of that, even while they re-emphasize the complexity and diversity of early Christian teaching.

Because of his opposition to Arianism Hilary of Poitiers (d. 367) spent a portion of his mature life as an exile in the eastern part of the empire. He was influenced by Cappadocian thought, and selections from his work on the Trinity express a view of salvation as divinization that is not to be found in an Ambrose or an Augustine. His "Christology" is sometimes described as "monophysite", but the use of these terms is anachronistic, and, since his major interest is trinitarian, in opposition to Arianism, one should not be surprised to find him stressing the savior's divinity.

For Ambrose (d. 397), who was not yet a baptized Christian when he was chosen bishop of Milan, the Son of God became flesh to save humanity, and it was through his death that he destroyed death and gave humanity the possibility of becoming immortal; the death of Jesus Christ is the center of Ambrose's understanding of Christian salvation. He often refers to these events and processes as "mysteries", but makes no real attempt to investigate their depths.

Augustine of Hippo (d. 430) is, of course, one of the most profound and influential thinkers of all time, but his teaching on Christ and salvation offers few surprises. One cannot but wonder how the history of the fifth century church would have developed, if Augustine had been able to attend the general council of Ephesus in 431,[1] for he touches upon almost all aspects of the issues at stake there, and his faith in the Word become flesh as one person, the Son of God who exists in two natures, is in harmony with the tradition that emerged from the councils of Ephesus and Chalcedon as mainstream orthodoxy. Augustine's understanding of salvation is colored by his theory of original sin and of human corruption: the savior's death, therefore, conquered death and the devil; the issue of God's justice and power arise, but not in the extreme form seen in Gregory of Nyssa.

In the middle of the fifth century, Leo, the bishop of Rome, published a document called the *Tome*, that played a major role in calming the controversy that raged, primarily in the East, up to that time. Leo will be mentioned again in the next chapter, but he will not be quoted in this volume, since the *Tome* is an official document issued in a polemical context for a specific occasion; it deals, therefore, with a limited range of topics and is not in keeping with the spirit of this collection. In any event, selections from Leo can be found in most of the collections dealing more specifically with the controversies and their resolutions.

---

[1] See the next chapter for more details on this council.

II. The Writings

1. HILARY OF POITIERS

On the Trinity

1. The virgin, the birth, the body, and later on, the cross, the death, and the lower world—these are our salvation. For the sake of the human race the Son of God was born of the virgin and the holy Spirit; he even ministered to himself in this process, for his own power, the power of God, overshadowed her (see Lk. 1.35), sowed the seeds of the body, and started the process resulting in the flesh. He did this so that he could become human through the virgin, and take the nature of flesh to himself, so that, through the association produced by this mixture, the body of the whole human race might be sanctified through him. As a result, just as all were hidden in him through the bodily reality that he chose to be, so he could be communicated to all through the invisible reality that he possessed. The invisible image of God (see Col. 1.15) did not, therefore, reject the shame involved in a human beginning, and he passed through the indignities to which our nature is subject, namely, conception, birth, crying, and cradle. (II.24)[2]

2. What can we possibly do, then, that would be a fitting return for such deep affection and esteem? The one, only begotten God, sprung from God in an ineffable way, is placed in the womb of the holy virgin and grows into the form of a small human body. The one who encompasses everything, and within whom and through whom all things exist, is brought forth in accordance with the laws of human birth. The one at whose voice archangels and angels tremble, and heaven, earth, and all the elements of this world are dissolved (see II Pt. 3.10 and 12), is heard when a baby cries. The one who is invisible and incomprehensible, who cannot be grasped by sign, sense, or touch, lies bundled in a cradle.

[2]Text of Book II: CCL, 62, 60-61.

Anyone who believes that this is unworthy of God will admit
to being more obliged for such a great gift, to the extent that
this is less consistent with God's majesty. The one through
whom the human being was made did not need to become a
human being; but we needed God to become flesh and to
dwell among us (see Jn. 1.14), that is, to dwell fully in all
flesh through the assumption of the flesh of one person. His
lowliness is our honor; his shame is our glory. Since he is
God living in flesh, we in turn are reconstituted, from flesh
to God. (II.25)

3. One has absolutely no knowledge of one's own life, if
one does not know that Jesus Christ is true God as well as a
true human being. And it is just as dangerous to deny that
Jesus Christ is divine Spirit as to deny that he is flesh of our
body. "Everyone, therefore, who will proclaim me before
human beings, I shall proclaim before my father who is in
heaven. But anyone who denies me before human beings, I
shall also deny before my father who is heaven" (Mt. 10.32-
33). This is what the Word made flesh said, and what the
human Jesus Christ, the lord of glory (see I Cor. 2.8), taught;
he was, in his own person, constituted mediator for the salvation of the church, and by virtue of that very mystery of
being mediator between God and humans (see I Tim. 2.5), he
is one person, but both God and human. Since both natures
have been united for this purpose, he is the full reality of
them both, and in such a way that he is in both, but lacks
nothing of either, lest he should cease to be God when born
as a human, or be any the less human because he continues
to be God. This, then, is the true faith that leads to human
blessedness: to declare that he is both God and a human
being; to confess that he is Word and flesh; not to be
unaware that he is God, because he is also a human, and not
to be ignorant of the flesh because he is Word. (IX.3)[3]

4. It is contrary to the nature of our experience for him to
be born as a human while remaining God, but it is not
contrary to the nature of our hope for him to remain God

[3]Text of Book IX: CCL, 62A, 373-384.

after being born as a human; for the birth of a higher nature into a lower one makes credible the possibility of a lower nature's being born into a higher one. The assumption of our nature does not represent progress for God, but the ignominy God freely chose is an advancement for us: God does not lose the reality of being God, but acquires for the human being the power to be God. (IX.4)

5. These, then, are the secret heavenly mysteries, established before the foundation of the world: the only begotten God willed to be born as a human, and the human was to remain forever in God; God willed to suffer, so that the devil, who raged against the natural effects of our weakness, would not be able to maintain the law of sin against us, because God assumed our suffering; God willed to die, so that, because the immortal God was freely subjected to the law of death, no proud power could rise against God or misuse the natural power created in it by God. God is, therefore, born to assume us, suffers to justify us, and finally dies to avenge us; when our humanity abides with God, the natural effects of our weaknesses are united to God, and the spiritual powers of evil and wickedness are subjected to the triumph of the flesh—for God died through the flesh (see Col. 2.15). [IX.7]

6. The apostle [Paul] was, therefore, aware of this mystery and had acquired knowledge of the faith through the lord himself; since he knew that this world, human beings, and philosophy could not grasp him, he said,

> Take care that no one seduce you through philosophy and empty deceit, in accordance with human traditions and worldly elements, and not according to Christ; for the whole fullness of divinity dwells in him bodily, and you have been filled in him, for he is the head of authority and power (Col. 2.8-10).

And so, after explaining that the fullness of divinity dwells in him bodily, he immediately went on to the mystery of our assumption by saying, "You have been filled through him."

For just as the fullness of divinity is in him, so we have been filled through him. He does not say, "You have been filled," but "You have been filled through him." He said this because all those who have been, or are to be, reborn, through the hope of faith in eternal life, have now been filled through, and abide in, the body of Christ, and later on will be filled, not through him, but through themselves, at that time of which the apostle says, "Who will transform the body of our lowliness into the form of the body of his glory"(Phil. 3.21). Now, therefore, we have been filled through him, that is, through the assumption of his flesh, in which the fullness of divinity dwells bodily; and the power of this hope we have in him is no small thing. (IX.8)

7. After presenting the mystery of his nature and the assumption of ours, seen in the fact that the fullness of divinity dwells in him and that we are filled through him because he was born a human being, [Paul] goes on to the rest of the divine plan for human salvation and says,

> In whom you also have been circumcised with a circumcision not done by hand through the removal of the body of flesh; but through the circumcision of Christ you were buried with him in baptism, through which you also rose with him through faith in the action of God who raised him from the dead" (Col. 2.11-12).

We are circumcised, therefore, not with a bodily circumcision, but with the circumcision of Christ; in other words, we have been born again into a new human being. For when we are buried with his baptism, we must die to the old human, because the rebirth of baptism is the power of the resurrection (see Rom. 6.4-6). This, then, is the circumcision of Christ—not to be deprived of a fleshly foreskin, but to die fully with him, and through this to live fully with him afterwards. For through him we rise, through faith in his God who raised him from the dead. We must, therefore, believe God, through whose action Christ was raised from the dead, since that faith rises through Christ. (IX.9)

8. In this way, then, the whole mystery of the assumption of humanity is completed.

> And when you were dead in sin and in your flesh's lack of circumcision, God gave life with him, forgave you all your sins, and cancelled the bond that was against us with its pronouncements; he put away whatever was hostile to us, and fixed it to the cross; stripped of his flesh, he made a display of the powers, after triumphing over them through himself (Col. 2.13-15).

A worldly person cannot grasp the faith taught by the apostle, nor can language other than his own explain the meaning of what he says. God raises Christ from the dead, that very Christ in whom the fullness of divinity dwells bodily. But God has given us life with him, forgiving our sins and cancelling the bond of the law of sin, which stood against us because of earlier pronouncements; God took this away and fixed it to the cross, stripping himself of flesh through the law of death and putting the powers on display, after triumphing over them through himself.

But who can understand or express this mystery? God's action raises Christ from the dead, and the same action of God gives us life with Christ; this same action forgives sins, cancels the bond, fixes it to the cross, strips himself of flesh, puts the powers on display, and triumphs over them through himself. You have the action of God who raises Christ from the dead, and you have Christ who performs through himself those very same actions that God performs. For Christ stripped himself of flesh and died. Hold on, then, to Christ, the human being, who was raised by God from the dead; hold on to Christ, the God, who performed the actions of our salvation when he was to die. When God does this in Christ, although it is God who is acting, it is nonetheless Christ who strips himself of flesh and dies; and when Christ died, he worked as God before his death, and yet it was the power of God that raised the dead Christ. The one who raised Christ from the dead is the same Christ who worked before his death and who stripped himself of flesh when he was to die. (IX.10)

9. Do you perceive him as he triumphs over the powers in himself? Do you see that there is no difference between the flesh that was stripped off and the one who strips the flesh from himself? For he triumphs in himself, that is, in that flesh of which he stripped himself. Do you see that in this way he is proclaimed as God and a human being, so that death is attributed to the human being, while the raising of the flesh is attributed to God, although not in such a way that the one who died and the one through whom the dead person rose are two different persons? For the stripped off flesh is the dead Christ, and the one who raises Christ from the dead is the same Christ who strips himself of the flesh. See the nature of God in the power to raise from the dead, and recognize the fate of the human in the death. Although both activities spring from their proper natures, remember that it is one Jesus Christ who is both. (IX. 11)

10. The blessed apostle took special note of the double reality in Christ, so as to teach that in him were the weakness of a human and the power and nature of God; thus he said to the Corinthians, "For although he was crucified through weakness, he lives through the power of God" (II Cor. 13.4), and so he shows that death is due to weakness, but life to the power of God. To the Romans he said, "Insofar as he died, he died once to sin; but insofar as he lives, he lives to God. But you, consider youselves as dead to sin, but alive to God through Christ Jesus" (Rom. 6.10-11); he ascribes death to sin, that is, to our body, and life to God, for whom living is natural. He says, therefore, that we must die to our body, in order to live for God through Christ Jesus, who assumed the body of our sin and now lives wholly for God; and through his sharing of our nature it has been united to, and participates in the divine immortality. (IX.13)

2. AMBROSE OF MILAN

On the Death of His Brother

1. [Jesus] wept, not for his state, but for ours; and since the divinity does not weep, he wept through that one who was sad; he wept through that one who was crucified, who died, and who was buried; he wept in that one of whom the prophet has today [in the reading just heard] reminded us in the words, "A human being will say, 'Mother Sion,' and a human being was made in her, and the most high himself has established her" (Ps. 87.5). He wept in that one through whom he said, "Mother Sion," since he was born in Judea and had been begotten by a virgin, although due to his divinity he could not have a mother, since he is the maker of the mother. He "was made" through a process of generation that was human, not divine, for "a human being was made," but God was born. (I.11)[4]

2. And so you read elsewhere, "A child is born for us, a son has been given to us" (Is. 9.6), for the idea of age is in the child, while in the son is "the fullness of divinity" (Col. 2.9). Made from a mother and born of a father, the same one has, nonetheless, been both born and given. You should picture one reality, not diversity; for one Son of God is both born of the Father and sprung from the virgin, in a different order, and yet comes together in one name, as the reading we just heard also teaches: for "a human being has been made in her, and the most high himself has established her"—"a human being," of course, because of the body, and "most high" because of the power. Although God and a human being because of the different natures, he is nonetheless one and the same person, not two persons because of the natures. One aspect of his nature, therefore, is special, and another is shared with us; but he is one person in both and perfect in both. It is, therefore, no surprise that "God made him lord and Christ" (Acts 2.36). [I.12-13][5]

[4]Text: CSEL, 73, 214-215.
[5]Text: CSEL, 73, 215-216.

3. What more is there to say? The world was redeemed through the death of one person. For Christ could have avoided death, if he had not wished to die; but he did not think that one should shrink from death, as though it were something shameful, nor could he have helped us more in any other way than through his own death. His death is, therefore, the life of all. We are marked by his death; when we pray, we announce his death; when we present offerings, we proclaim his death. His death is victory; his death is a sacrament; his death is an annual ritual observance for the world. What, moreover, could we say about his death, when we prove, through a divine example, that death by itself has achieved immortality, and that death itself has redeemed itself? One should not, therefore, grieve for death, which brings about the salvation of all; one should not flee from death, which the Son of God did not flee from or spurn. The order of nature is not to be destroyed; for there can be no exceptions for individuals in the case of something which is common to all. (II.46)[6]

On the Sacrament of the Lord's Becoming Flesh

4. He was, therefore, immortal in death and incapable of suffering even as he suffered; for the affliction of death did not grasp him since he was God, and at the same time the lower world saw him since he was a human being. In the end "he gave up his spirit" (Mt. 27.50), but he gave it up like one who is in charge of laying down and assuming a body, and so he did not lose the spirit. He hung on the cross and moved everything; he, before whom the whole world trembled, trembled on the tree; he was tortured, he received wounds, and he gave the gift of the heavenly kingdom; he became the sin of all and washed away the sins of the human race. Finally he died—and for the second and third time, with joy and exultation, I say, "he died"—so that his death might become the life of those who have died. (5.39)[7]

[6]Text: CSEL, 73, 273.
[7]Text: CSEL, 79, 242-243.

5. You have learned, therefore, that he offered a sacrifice from our reality. For what other reason was there for becoming flesh than to have the flesh, which had sinned, be redeemed through itself. That which had sinned, therefore, was redeemed. But the divinity of the Word was not sacrificed, since the divinity of the Word had not sinned. And the nature of the Word was not, then, changed into the nature of flesh, because the divinity was free of sin and did not have to offer itself for sin, which it had not committed. For Christ offered in himself what he put on, and he put on what he did not have before. The one who possessed "the fullness of eternal divinity" (Col. 2.9) did not, therefore, put on the divinity of his own divine nature; he assumed flesh, in order to lay aside the covering that is the flesh, to crucify in himself the devil's booty, and to raise up the trophies of virtue. (6.56)[8]

6. When he took on the flesh of a human being, it follows that he took on the perfection and plenitude of becoming flesh; for there is nothing imperfect in Christ. And so he took on flesh, in order to raise it again; he assumed a soul, but he assumed and took on a perfect, human, and rational soul. I say that he took on [a soul], for the Word of God did not become live in its flesh by replacing our soul; the Word, rather, assumed both our flesh and our soul by assuming human nature perfectly. He assumed the soul, I say, in order to bless it with the sacrament of his becoming flesh; he took on my emotions and feelings in order to cure them. But why should he take on flesh without a soul, since it is certain that non-intelligent flesh and the irrational soul are neither guilty of sin nor deserving of reward? He took on for us, therefore, that which was in greater danger. What good does it do, however, if he did not redeem me totally? But the one who says, "Are you angry with me, who healed a man totally on the sabbath?" (Jn. 7.23) did redeem me totally. He redeemed me totally, because the one who is faithful rises "into a per-

fect man" (Eph. 4.13) totally, and not in part. (7.65-68)[9]

7. God the Word was not in its flesh to replace the soul that is rational and capable of understanding; God the Word took on both a soul that is rational and capable of understanding, human, and of the same substance as our souls, and flesh that is like ours and of the same substance as ours, and thus became a perfect human being, but without any stain of sin; for "he committed no sin" (I Pt. 2.22), but became sin for us, that we might be the righteousness of God through him (see II Cor. 5.21). His flesh and soul, therefore, are of the same substance as our soul and flesh. (7.76)[10]

On the Faith

8. It is because of the body, that is, because of us, that he was hungry; it is because of the body that he wept and that he was sad unto death (see Mt. 4.2; Jn. 11.35; Mt. 26.38). Why are attributes that are ours referred to the divinity? It is also because of the body that he is said to have been made (see Jn. 1.14); finally you have this: "A human being will say, 'Mother Sion,' and a human being was made in her, and the most high himself has established her" (Ps. 87.5). It says, "a human being was made," not, "God was made." Who, then, is at the same time "the most high" and "a human being," if not "the mediator between God and human beings, Jesus Christ, the human being, who gave himself once and for all as a redemption for us?" (I Tim. 2.5-6). This obviously refers to his becoming flesh, for our redemption was effected through blood, forgiveness was granted through power, and life was given through grace. He gives as "the most high," and he prays as "a human being" (see Mt. 11.25, 26.39-44, 27.46; Lk. 23.46; Jn. 17.1); the first work is that of the creator, and the second that of the redeemer. Although these acts of favor are distinct from one another, they come from one source; for it was proper for the one who created us to

[9]Text: CSEL, 79, 258-259.
[10]Text: CSEL, 79, 262-263.

redeem us (see Heb. 2.10). (III.2.7-8)[11]

9. "Being made" does not always refer to creation, for it was written, "Lord, you have been made a refuge for us" (Ps. 90.1), and, "You have been made a salvation for me" (see Ps. 118.14). This is obviously not a declaration defining or proclaiming a creation; God is said to have "been made a refuge" for me and to have turned "to me" for the sake of salvation, just as the apostle said, "who was made for us, through God, wisdom, righteousness, sanctification, and redemption" (I Cor. 1.30). He said, "was made for us," not "created through the Father." Finally he explained later on what he meant by saying that "he was made wisdom for us":

> But we are speaking of the wisdom of God in a mystery; that wisdom was hidden, and God predestined it before the time of the world for our glory, and none of the princes of this world knew it. For if they had known it, they would never have crucified the lord of glory (I Cor. 2.7-8).

When the term "mystery" is used of the passion, he is surely not proclaiming a process of eternal generation. The lord's cross is, therefore, my wisdom; the lord's death is my redemption. For we have been redeemed by "a precious blood" (I Pt. 1.19), as the apostle Peter said. The lord redeemed us through his blood, as a human being, therefore, and the same lord, as God, has forgiven sins (see Mk. 2.8-12). (III.5.35-36)[12]

10. The following words were written about the lord's becoming flesh: "The lord created me as the beginning of his ways for his works" (Prov. 8.22); we have understood them to mean that the lord Jesus was created from the virgin to redeem the Father's works. There can be no doubt that this was said about the mystery of his becoming flesh, because, "for his works," which were to be freed from slavery to

[11]Text: CSEL, 78, 110-111.
[12]Text: CSEL, 78, 120-121.

corruption, the lord took on flesh, in order "to destroy," through his bodily suffering, "the one who held the power of death" (see Heb. 2.14). For Christ's flesh exists on account of "the works," while the divinity existed before the works, because "he exists before everything, and everything exists through him" (Col. 1.17). [III.7.46][13]

11. According to the church's faith, one and the same person is Son of God the Father and son of David; for the mystery of God's becoming flesh is the salvation of all creation, as it says in scripture, "So that without God he might taste death for all" (Heb. 2.9). In other words, every creature, without any suffering by the divinity, is to be redeemed at the price of the lord's blood, as it says elsewhere, "Every creature will be freed from slavery to corruption" (Rom. 8.21). It is one thing, therefore, to be called a Son on account of the divine substance, and another to be called son due to the assumption of the flesh. The Son is equal to God the Father because of divine generation, and is a servant of God the Father because of the assumption of a body; for it says, "he took the form of a servant" (Phil. 2.7). But it is one and the same Son. (V.8.106-107)[14]

On the Holy Spirit[15]

12. The Father, therefore, is spirit, and the Son is spirit, for anything that is not a created body is spirit. And yet the holy Spirit is not combined with the Father and the Son, but is distinct from the Father and the Son. For the holy Spirit did not die, because it cannot die, since it did not assume flesh, and "eternal divinity" (Rom. 1.20) cannot be susceptible to death. But Christ died in the flesh, and he surely died through what he assumed from the virgin, not through what he had from the Father. For Christ died through that through which he was crucified. The holy Spirit, however, cannot be crucified, because it did not have flesh and bones

[13]Text: CSEL, 78, 124-125.
[14]Text: CSEL, 78, 255.
[15]Text: CSEL, 79, 61-63.

(see Lk. 24.39). But the Son of God, who took on flesh and bones, so that the temptations of our flesh might die on that cross, was crucified. For he assumed what he was not, in order to hide what he was; he hid what he was, so that what he was not might be tempted and redeemed through him— he did this so that he might call us to that which he was through that which he was not. (I.9.106-107)

13. O divine mystery of that cross, on which weakness hangs, power is free, vices are nailed, and victory trophies are raised up. For this reason a holy man says, "Pierce my flesh with nails through fear of you" (see Ps. 119.120 [LXX,118.120]); he does not mean nails of iron, but of fear and of faith. For the bondage of virtue is stronger than that of punishment. Finally, when Peter followed the lord "into the courtyard of the priests" (see Mt. 26.58), his faith bound him whom no one had bound (see Mt. 26.75?), and punishment did not free him whom faith had bound; later on, when he was bound by the Jews, prayer released him, and punishment did not hold him, because he did not draw away from Christ (see Acts 12.3-17). (I.9.108)

14. Crucify sin yourself, therefore, that you may die to sin. For anyone who dies to sin, lives to God (see Rom. 6.10-11). May you live for the one, "who did not spare his own son" (Rom. 8.32), in order to crucify our passions in his body (see Gal. 5.24). For "Christ died for us" (see Rom. 5.8), that we might live through his body which was restored to life. Not our life, therefore, but our guilt died through him. It says, "Who bore our sins in his own body on the tree, so that we might be separated from our sins and live with righteousness; and you have been healed by his wounds" (I Pt. 2.24). That tree, therefore, a ship of our salvation, as it were, is our means of passage, not a punishment, for salvation is something distinct from the means of passage to eternal salvation. In seeking death I do not feel it; in despising punishment I do not suffer; in ignoring fear I do not know it. (I.9.109-110)

15. Who, then, is the one through whose wounds we have been healed (see I Pt. 2.24)? It is Christ the lord, about whom Isaiah prophesied that the blows he received were

medicine for us (see Is. 53.5), and about whom the apostle Paul wrote in his letters, "that he did not know sin, but was made sin for us" (II Cor. 5.21). And this was a certain sign of his divinity: his flesh did not commit sin, and the created body assumed by him did not sin. For what would be strange about the divinity by itself not sinning, when it has no inclination toward sin? But if God alone is exempt from sin, every creature, by its very nature, as we have said, can certainly fall into sin. (I.9.111)

On Repentance[16]

16. How can your sacrifice be acceptable to God, when you deny mercy, even though God claims to will, not the death, but the amendment of the sinner (see Ezek. 33.11)? The apostle is interpreting this when he says, "God, sending his own son in the likeness of the flesh of sin and as a sin-offering, condemned sin in the flesh, so that the justification of the law might be fulfilled in us" (Rom. 8.3-4). He does not say, "in the likeness of flesh," because Christ assumed true human flesh, not a likeness of it; nor does he say, "in the likeness of sin," because "he did not commit sin" (I Pt. 2.22), but became sin for us (see II Cor. 5.21). He came instead "in the likeness of the flesh of sin"; in other words, he assumed the likeness of sinful flesh. He used "likeness," therefore, because it was written, "He is a human being, and who knows him?" (Jer. 17.9 [LXX]). In keeping with his humanity he was a human being in the flesh, in order to be known; but in power he was beyond the human and was not known. And so he had our flesh, but did not have the vices of this flesh. (I.3.11-12)

17. For he was not begotten, as all human beings are, through the union of a man and a woman, but was born of the holy Spirit and the virgin, and assumed a stainless body, which was not only absolutely free from the stain of vice, but had also not been blackened through the harmful formation

that is generation and conception. For all of us human beings are born in sin, and our beginnings are rooted in vice, as you can read in the words of David, "For behold I was conceived in iniquities, and in sin my mother begot me" (Ps. 51.5). Paul's flesh, therefore, was the body of death, as he says himself, "Who will free me from the body of this death?" (Rom. 7.24). But the flesh of Christ condemned sin, which he did not experience at his birth, and which he crucified through his death, so that there might be justification through grace in our flesh, where before there was contamination through guilt. (I.3.13)

18. "What, then, shall we say to this" other than what the apostle said?

> If God is for us, who is against us? God did not spare his own son, but handed him over for all of us—did God not also give us everything else along with him? Who will make an accusation against God's chosen ones? God, who justifies? Who will condemn? Christ, who died, and who also rose, and is at God's right hand, and who intercedes for us (Rom. 8.31-34)?

Those people, therefore, for whom Christ intercedes, Novatian condemns. The people whom Christ redeemed to salvation, Novatian condemns to death. (I.3.14)

19. [In his own words, Jesus] promises grace to all people, but does not threaten punishment on all. He emphasizes the attributes of mercy, but plays down those of vengeance (see Mt. 10.28, 32-33). (I.4.16)

3. AUGUSTINE

On the Gift of Perseverance[17]

1. There is no more glorious example of predestination than Jesus himself. There is, I say, no more glorious example

[17]Text: PL, 45.1033-1034.

of predestination than the mediator himself. Any believer who wishes to understand predestination well, should concentrate on him and he would even find himself in him; I am referring to any believer who believes and confesses that, in him, a true human nature (that is to say, our nature, even though the divine Word assumed it in a unique way) was raised into the only Son of God in such a way, that the one who assumed and what that one assumed were one person in the trinity. For with the assumption of the human being the trinity did not become a quaternity, but remained what it was, and that assumption produced, in a mysterious way, the reality of one person in God and a human being.

We do not say that Christ is only God, as the heretical Manichaeans do; we do not say that he is only a human being, as do the heretical Photinians; nor do we say that he is a human being in such a way as to lack something which clearly belongs to human nature, as for example, a soul, or a rational mind in that very soul, or flesh, not taken from a woman, but produced from the Word transformed and changed into flesh. These three erroneous and empty opinions have resulted in three separate and distinct types of Apollinarian heretics. But we say that Christ is true God, born of God the Father with no beginning in time; we also say that the same person is a true human being, born of a human mother at the fixed fullness of time; we do not say that his humanity, because of which he is inferior to the Father, in any way diminishes his divinity, because of which he is equal to the Father. This double reality is one Christ— as God he has said most truly, "I and the father are one" (Jn. 10.30); as a human being he has also said most truly, "The father is greater than I" (Jn. 14.28). (67)

City of God[18]

2. "A heavy yoke is on the sons of Adam from the day they left their mothers' wombs until the day of their burial in the mother of all" (Sir. 40.1); these words of scripture must

---

[18]Text: *Augustine. City of God,* VII (Loeb), 82-90.

be fulfilled in such a way that even little children who have, through the washing of rebirth, been freed from the bonds of original sin which alone held them captive, suffer many evils, and so some of them at times even suffer the attacks of evil spirits. But it is unthinkable that this suffering should injure them, even if their lives end at that age because the suffering grows worse and drives the soul from the body. (XXI.14)

3. With respect, however, to the "heavy yoke" which has been placed "on the sons of Adam from the day they left their mothers' wombs until the day of their burial in the mother of all," even this evil appears remarkable. Through it, therefore, we learn to be sensible and to realize that this life, because of that horrible sin which was committed in paradise, has become our punishment, and that all that is done on our behalf through the new covenant pertains only to the inheritance of the new age, so that we, who have received a pledge here, might in its own proper time achieve the reality that was pledged. But in the meantime we are to walk in hope and must progress day by day, putting the works of the flesh to death through the spirit (see Rom. 8.13). For "the lord knows those who are his" (II Tim. 2.19), and "all who are led by God's spirit are sons of God" (Rom. 8.14)—but they are sons of God by grace, not by nature.

For the only Son of God by nature became a son of man, out of pity for us, so that we who were sons of man by nature might, through him, become sons of God by grace. While remaining unchangeable, he assumed from us our nature, so that he could assume us through it. While holding on to his divinity, he came to share in our weakness, so that we might change for the better, through our participation in his immortality and righteousness, by shedding what is sinful and mortal in us and preserving the good which he did through our nature, after that good had been filled with the highest good through the goodness of his nature. For just as we fell into such a terrible evil as this through the sin of one human, so , through the righteousness given by one human who was also God, shall we reach that good which is so exalted (see Rom. 5.15).

No one should be confident of having passed from one state to the other, before arriving where there is no temptation, and before winning the peace sought in the many different battles of this war, in which "flesh lusts against spirit and spirit against flesh"(Gal. 5.17). But this war would never have taken place if human nature, through free will, had stood firm in the righteousness in which it was created. As things are, this nature, which would not stay at peace with God and be happy, is now unhappy and at war with itself; and even though this is a miserable and evil condition, it is nonetheless better than the way this life formerly was. For it is better to do battle with vices than to fall under their control without a struggle. Better, I say, is war with a hope of peace, than captivity that admits no thought of liberation. We hope indeed to be rid of this war, and we are inflamed by the fire of divine love to grasp for a truly well-ordered peace, where lower things are subjected to higher with unchanging stability. But if, God forbid, there were no hope of such a great good as this, then we should have preferred to continue in the trials of this conflict than to have allowed our vices to rule us because of our failure to resist them. (XXI.15)

4. God's mercy toward "the vessels of mercy which he has prepared in advance for glory" (Rom. 9.23) is so great that it touches even the first age of a human being, that is, infancy, which is subject to flesh without any resistance. It also touches the second age, which is called childhood, in which the power of reason has not yet taken up this battle and is almost at the mercy of every evil pleasure; for although childhood can speak and appears to have transcended infancy, its weakness of mind is not yet capable of observing God's commandment. God's mercy, however, is so great that, if one has received the sacraments of the mediator, even though one should die during these early years, one would be brought from the power of darkness to the kingdom of Christ, so that one would not only not be faced with eternal punishment, but would not even undergo any cleansing suffering after death. For spiritual rebirth is by itself strong enough to prevent, after death, any of the evils brought on,

along with death, by fleshly birth. But when one reaches the age at which one understands the commandments and can be subject to the rule of law, then one must declare war upon vice and wage it fiercely, to avoid falling into sins that merit condemnation. If the vices have not yet been strengthened by habitual victory, they are easily overcome and they yield; but if they have grown accustomed to victory and domination, then it requires hard and difficult work to overcome them.

This can only be done truly and seriously when one takes pleasure in true righteousness, which consists in faith in Christ. For if the law is there giving commands, but the Spirit is not there to help, then the desire for sin grows and conquers, until one is also guilty of transgression. Sometimes, of course, the most obvious vices are overcome by other, secret vices, which are thought to be virtues; pride is the main one of these, along with destructive haughtiness that seeks to please itself. Vices may be considered overcome, therefore, only when they are conquered by love of God; this love is a gift of no one else but God, and it is given only through "the mediator between God and humans, the human Jesus Christ" (I Tim. 2.5), who took up a share in our mortality, so that he could make us share in his divinity. (XXI.16)

On the Trinity[19]

5. What does "justified by his blood" (Rom. 5.9) mean? I ask you, what power does this blood have so that believers are justified by it? And what does "reconciled by the death of his son" (Rom. 5.10) mean? Does it mean that, when God the Father was angry with us, he saw his Son's death for us and became kindly disposed toward us? It surely could not have meant that his Son was already so well disposed toward us that he would even be willing to die for us, while the Father, on the other hand, was still so angry, that he would never be appeased, unless his Son died for us. And what is

---

[19]Text: PL, 42.1025-1029.

the meaning of the following statement which the very same teacher of the gentiles made elsewhere? "What shall we, therefore, say to this? If God is for us, who is against us? How can the one who did not spare his very own son, but handed him over for all of us, not have given us everything else along with him?" (Rom. 8.31-32). If the Father had not already been appeased, would he have given up his own Son and handed him over for us? But this idea seems to contradict the other one. In the first case, the Son dies for us, and the Father is reconciled to us through his death; here, however, since the Father already loved us, he does not spare his own Son because of us, but hands him over to death on our behalf.

But I see that the Father loved us even before this; he loved us, not only before the Son died for us, but even before he created the world. The apostle himself testifies to this, when he says, "As he chose us in him before the foundation of the world" (Eph. 1.4). Nor was the Son handed over for us as though against his will, because his Father did not spare him; for it was said about him, "who loved me and handed himself over for me" (Gal. 2.20). The Father, the Son, and the Spirit of both of them, therefore, do all things together in an equal and harmonious way; but we are nevertheless justified by the blood of Christ and reconciled to the Father through the death of his Son. I shall explain here, to the best of my ability and as extensively as possible, how this took place. (XIII.XI.15)

6. God's justice delivered the human race into the power of the devil, because the sin of the first human being passed on from the beginning to all those who were born as a result of sexual intercourse, and because the debt of the first parents bound all their descendants. But the way in which humanity was delivered into the devil's power is not to be understood as implying that God did this or ordered it to be done; God only permitted it, and acted justly in doing so. For when God abandoned the sinner, the originator of sin marched in there. God did not, of course, abandon his creature in such a way, as not to appear to it as a God who

creates and gives life, and who bestows many good things, even on evil people, in the midst of evils which come as punishment; for in anger God has not held back mercy (see Ps. 77.9 [LXX,76.10]). God did not release humanity from the law of God's power, in allowing it to be in the devil's power, because even the devil is not independent, either of the almighty's power, or, in the same way, of goodness. For how could evil angels exist in any way at all, except through the one who gives life to everything? If, therefore, the committing of sins subjected humanity to the devil through God's just anger, then the remission of sins through a loving reconciliation with God surely tears humanity away from the devil. (XIII.XII.16)

7. The devil was to be conquered, however, not by God's power, but by justice. For what is more powerful than the almighty one? What creature's power can be compared to the power of the creator? But the devil, through his own wicked perversity, fell in love with power, abandoned justice, and fought against it; and human beings also imitate the devil in this, in direct proportion to the way in which they neglect, or even hate justice and strive after power, and in proportion to the pleasure they have in acquiring power or to the extent that they are inflamed with lust for it. Because of all this, God decided that, to rescue humanity from the devil's power, the devil should be conquered by justice, not by power, and that human beings should also imitate Christ in this, and seek to conquer the devil by justice, not by power. (XIII.XIII.17)

8. What is the justice, then, by which the devil was conquered? What else but the justice of Jesus Christ? How was he conquered? The devil was conquered, because, even though he found in Jesus nothing that deserved death, he nonetheless killed him. And it is certainly just for the debtors whom the devil held to be declared free, because they believed in the one whom the devil killed, even though he had no debt. This is what it means when we are said to be "justified by the blood" of Christ (see Rom. 5.9). For that innocent blood was shed in this way for the remission of our

sins. It says in the psalms, therefore, that he is "free among the dead" (see Ps. 88.5 [LXX, 87.5]); for only one who is dead is free from the debt of death. And in another psalm it says, "Shall I now pay back what I did not take? (see Ps. 69.4 [LXX, 68.5]). It wanted this taking to stand for sin, because it took illegitimately. Through the mouth of his own flesh, therefore, as one reads in the gospel, he says, "Behold the ruler of this world is coming and finds nothing in me," that is to say, no sin; "but that all may know that I do my father's will, arise, and let us go away from here" (Jn. 14.30-31). And he then goes on to the passion, in order to pay for us debtors what he himself did not owe.

The devil would not have been overcome by this very just sanction, if Christ had wished to deal with him through power instead of justice. But Christ put off doing what he had the power to do, in order to do first that which he had to do. He, therefore, had to be both a human being and God. If he had not been human, he could not have been put to death; if he had not been God, no one would have believed that he did not want to do what he could do; they would have thought rather that he could not do what he wanted to do; and we would not have thought that he preferred justice to power, but simply that he lacked power. But the fact is that he endured human sufferings for us because he was human; and if he had been unwilling to do so, he could not even have suffered this, because he was also God. His justice, therefore, became more pleasing because of his humiliation, for the power of his divinity was such that it could not have suffered humiliation if he had not willed it. And so, this powerful person, by dying, bestowed justice on, and promised power to us powerless mortals. He did the former by dying, and the latter by rising from the dead. For what is more just than going as far as death on a cross on behalf of justice? And what is more powerful than rising from the dead and ascending into heaven with the very flesh in which one was killed?

He conquered the devil, therefore, first by justice and then by power. He did it by justice, because he had no sin and was most unjustly killed by the devil; but he also did it by power, because he came back to life after dying, never to die again (see Rom. 6.9). He would have conquered the devil by power, even if he could not have been killed by him; but it is a mark of greater power to conquer death itself by rising, than to avoid it by living. But there is another reason for which we are justified by the blood of Christ, when we are snatched from the devil's power through the remission of sins; it consists in the fact that Christ conquers the devil through justice, not power. For Christ was crucified because of the weakness he assumed through mortal flesh, not through the immortal power, although Paul says of this weakness, "What is weakness for God is stronger than humans" (I Cor. 1.25). (XIII.XIV.18)

9. It is not difficult, therefore, to see that the devil was conquered, when the one whom he killed rose from the dead. But seeing that the devil is conquered just when he thought that he had conquered, that is, when Christ was killed, is a greater thing and more difficult to understand. For at that moment, since that blood belonged to the one who had no sin at all, it was poured out for the remission of our sins; as a result, because the devil had the right to hold captive those who were guilty of sin and whom he, therefore, bound in the state of death, it was also right for him to free these people through the one who was guilty of no sin, but whom he undeservedly afflicted with the punishment of death. The "strong man" (see Mk. 3.27) is conquered by this justice and bound by this chain, so that his vessels, which in the case of the devil and his angels were vessels of wrath, were taken away and turned into vessels of mercy (see Rom. 9.22-23).

The apostle Paul tells how these words of our lord Jesus Christ himself were spoken to him from heaven, when he was first called; for among other things that he heard, he says that the following was also said to him:

> For I have appeared to you for this reason, to establish you as a servant, and as a witness of the things which you see from me, and in which I also appear to you, freeing you from

the people and from the gentiles to whom I send you, to open the eyes of the blind, that they may turn from darkness and from the power of satan to God, in order to receive the remission of sins, a share among the holy ones, and the faith which is in me (see Acts 26.16-18).

The same apostle, therefore, also urges believers to thank God the Father, and says, "Because he has snatched us from the power of darkness and brought us to the kingdom of the son whom he loves, through whom we have redemption for the remission of sins" (Col. 1.13-14).

In this redemption the blood of Christ was given for us as a price, and when the devil took it, he was bound, not enriched; it was given so that we might be freed from his bonds, and that he might not trap in the nets of sin, and so drag with him to the destruction of the second, eternal death, any of those whom Christ had redeemed from all debt by shedding his blood freely and without any need to do so. And the final result was that those who are associated with Christ's grace, foreknown, predestined, and chosen before the foundation of the world, may die only to the extent that Christ himself died for them, with the death merely of the flesh, not of the spirit. (XIII.XV.19)

Chapter Six

Controversy and Consolidation

I. Introduction

Theodore of Mopsuestia (d. 428) bridged the fourth and
fifth centuries by his influence as well as by the dates of his
life. He was a contemporary of John Chrysostom, whom he
outlived by over twenty years, and he was mentioned in a
previous chapter in connection with Gregory of Nyssa.[1] Like
Chrysostom, Theodore studied in Antioch, and his theology
is usually classified as belonging to that tradition; his roots
are, therefore, in the fourth century, but for the purposes of
this volume he is better placed with the authors of the fifth.
During his lifetime Theodore was revered as a saint and as
the premier scriptural exegete of his day. His reputation suffered after his death, primarily because of the controversy
surrounding the teaching of Nestorius, who was considered a
notorious heretic; since Theodore apparently influenced Nestorius, he is often called an ancestor of the latter's heresy. As
a result, this man who was so admired during his lifetime was
vilified after his death, and was condemned by a general
council at Constantinople over 100 years after his death (in
the year 553).

[1]See above, p. 93.

Theodore was, therefore, considered a heretic until well into the twentieth century, but his reputation for basic orthodoxy has been restored in the last several decades. Contemporary scholars tend to attribute many of the problems with Theodore's thought to his lack of linguistic and conceptual sophistication; in other words, he had not developed the categories to express his insights in a manner that would be acceptable to later generations. This could simply be another way of saying that Theodore was ahead of his time. It cannot be denied that there were, and still are problems with his thought as we read it in his extant works, at least in terms of its expression; but his general approach, which stresses the humanity of Christ and its role in the divinization of human nature, has found a sympathetic audience in the modern world. For that reason, and because Theodore was so well respected and so influential during his life, this anthology includes several lengthy selections from his so called catechetical homilies on the creed of the council of Nicaea.

Since he reached his maturity in the last quarter of the fourth century, Theodore was surely familiar with the teaching of Apollinarius of Laodicaea, who was condemned at the council of Constantinople in 381. The divinization of humanity, according to Apollinarius, was the result of a process which seemed to entail the complete absorption of Christ's humanity by his divine nature. Whether or not this evaluation of Apollinarius was correct, those who followed his lead did stress the divine nature of the savior; this approach was in line with a spirituality that centered on mystical union with God, and as such it had a great appeal. It also led, however, to a more extreme position in which it seemed that the humanity of the Christ disappeared completely.[2] The teaching of Apollinarius is traditionally associated with the thought of Alexandria, while the opposition is generally linked with the church of Antioch, of which Theodore is in many ways a typical example; Theodoret of Cyrus, who

---

[2] This position was condemned as the Monophysite heresy by a general council at Chalcedon in 451; see below under Theodoret and Cyril.

appears later in this chapter, and Nestorius, were in the same tradition as Theodore.

Although Theodore always stressed the divinity of the Word and the Christ against Arian survivals, he especially stressed the human reality of the Word become flesh, which is, according to him, the key to the salvation of all human beings. Not unlike Gregory of Nyssa, he seemed to detect a kind of growth or development in the human reality of the Christ, which culminated in its full divinization and glorification after the death and resurrection of Jesus; salvation consists in the sharing of this glorification with human beings who believe in Jesus the Christ. It seems likely that Theodore developed his ideas with reference to Apollinarius, and this would explain the emphasis on the need that the Christ's humanity had for perfection. If the Word become flesh was truly human and was to offer true perfection to fallen humanity, Theodore reasons, the Word become flesh had to go through the same process as those it would save. This theory was, unfortunately, understood as implying that Jesus Christ was not truly divine, since the divinity was perfect in itself and could admit of no further progression toward perfection.

Theodore's language does lack sophistication; he uses concrete terms where later tradition would use abstractions; calling the humanity of the Word become flesh the "man assumed by the Word," for example, can easily give rise to the belief that Theodore taught that the Word become flesh was the product of a union of two different persons, or sons, especially when he says that the person was son of God, not by nature, but by grace and the good favor of God. This was, in brief, the teaching attributed to Nestorius, which was condemned by a general council of Ephesus in 431 and is usually associated with the tradition of the church of Antioch. What has already been said should offer sufficient evidence that this was not Theodore's intent and that his thought can be interpreted in an orthodox way that pays serious attention to the importance of the Word's humanity, and that adds a further dimension to the rich complexity of the early Christian church's understanding of Christ and salvation.

Cyril (d. 444), was bishop of Alexandria and leader of the battle against Nestorius (who was bishop of Constantinople from 428) and the tradition in Antioch which, in Cyril's view, negated the divinity of Jesus, the Christ and savior, by dividing him into two sons or persons, one human and the other divine, who were joined in a loose union through God's good will or grace. Cyril was the central figure at the general council held at Ephesus in 431, and succeeded there in condemning Nestorius, removing him from office, and sending him into permanent exile. In earlier writings, such as his commentary on John's gospel, Cyril's language is not unlike that of his counterpart from Antioch, John Chrysostom,[3] but after coming into conflict with Nestorius, and especially after 431, the tone and content of his writings change radically. The letters he exchanged with Nestorius are among the primary sources for this controversy, but, since they are quasi-official documents and are quoted so frequently, this volume cites instead his letter to Successus and his *Scholia* on the incarnation, which are just as expressive of his mature thought, but are less polemical and do not appear so often in English.

One of the key items in the controversy between Cyril and Nestorius was the designation of Mary the virgin as "mother of God," which Nestorius rejected, on the grounds that it did away with the savior's humanity and possibly compromised his divinity; for Cyril, however, this title accentuated the savior's divinity, and it, therefore, became a touchstone of orthodoxy. The leading thinkers of the church in Antioch felt, accordingly, that Cyril's position was in the tradition of Apollinarius, and that it led, in its extreme forms, to Monophysitism, or a denial of the Christ's humanity. Cyril and his defenders, on the other hand, saw in their opponents a true Nestorianism, which denied the savior's divinity because of its refusal to admit that the Word who became flesh was united to that flesh in such a way as to form one person and one Son, the Son of God become flesh. The two sides dis-

[3]See chapter four.

puted continuously, despite several attempts at reconciliation, until a general council at Chalcedon in 451 provided what was intended to be a compromise solution. What was accepted peacefully in the West, however, caused further bitterness in the East, and the ensuing split grew for several hundred years and is still reflected today, if not in spirit, at least in the official position of churches which either accept or reject the teaching of the council of Chalcedon.

Theodoret (d. c. 466), bishop of Cyrus, was a tragic figure who began as a friendly supporter of Nestorius and opponent of Cyril; he was condemned as a heretic and troublemaker in 449 through the efforts of Dioscorus, Cyril's successor as bishop of Alexandria,[4] but was restored to good favor at the council of Chalcedon after repudiating Nestorius and all that he represented. A selection from Theodoret's treatise on divine providence places him in the tradition of Gregory of Nyssa on salvation as a despoiling of the devil, and of John Chrysostom and Theodore of Mopsuestia on the understanding of what it meant for the Word to become flesh. His letters reflect the changing fortunes noted above, and thus one sees him also accepting positions similar to Cyril's and refuting accusations of Nestorianism; the "festal letters" express the simple unanalyzed faith of the ordinary Christian in the Word who became flesh and died for human salvation.

Thedoret is often described as unimaginative and derivative, and as a time-server or a politician devoid of principle; in this context one could point to what he says in his letters to Irenaeus (16) and Dioscorus (83) about calling Mary the mother of God. He did not have the brilliance and creativity of a Cyril of Alexandria; but the shifts in his thought and allegiance are perhaps more a reflection of the political situation and of the fluid complexity of Christian thought in his day, than a sign of lack of conviction or principle on his part.

[4]Theodoret was condemned at a council held in the city of Ephesus in 449; its actions were rejected as unlawful at Chalcedon, and it came to be known as the "Robber Council".

In the final analysis, Leo, the bishop of Rome,[5] did apparently side with his position, and yet he was condemned; his rehabilitation at Chalcedon was contingent on his repudiating his friends and much of what he had personally believed and taught. And the council of Chalcedon, in the final analysis, did not bring peace or unity to the church.

Although the so-called creed of the council of Chalcedon is an official statement and is often quoted in anthologies, it will be cited here, as a closing document exemplifying the end of an era, in order to provide a basis of comparison with the various "messages" expressed by the early Christian writers.

II. The Writings

1. THEODORE OF MOPSUESTIA[6]

Third Catechetical Homily[7]

1. "And in one lord Jesus Christ, only Son of God and firstborn of all creatures." After teaching about the Father, [the fathers at Nicaea] had to instruct us next about the Son as well, according to the teaching of our lord. In speaking about the Father they did not simply say "father," in accordance with our lord's teaching, but added that "God the Father is one, the maker of everything." They placed the name of God first in the profession of faith, saying that he is one, in order to destroy the error of polytheism; then they said that he is "father and maker of everything." They did the same thing with respect to the Son, when they said, "in one lord Jesus Christ, only Son of God and firstborn of all

---

[5]For further information about Leo and his writings see the previous chapter.

[6]The translation is based on the French translation of the Syriac text in *Les homélies catéchétiques de Théodore de Mopsueste,* ed. R. Tonneau (ST, 145); paragraph numbers here correspond to those in Tonneau.

[7]Text: Tonneau, 53-73.

creatures"; these words put them in complete agreement with the teaching of Paul, who preached against images and idols in order to refute the error of polytheism by saying, "There is no God except one" (I Cor. 8.4).

2. Because Paul knew that we teach the confession of faith in the Father, the Son, and the holy Spirit, he took pains to help us understand clearly that the formula of confessing the individuals [in the trinity] does not harm our religion and does not involve us in the error of polytheism. Since we know that the divine nature of the Father, the Son, and the holy Spirit is one, Paul, who wished to teach us this faith succinctly, said, "For us, God the Father, from whom everything is, is one" (I Cor. 8.6). By saying that God the Father is one he destroys totally the error of polytheism and proclaims that we preach only one divine nature. And once he had introduced the person of the Father, then he also revealed the Son to us. For he went on to say, "The lord Jesus Christ, through whom everything is, is one" (I Cor. 8.6). He said this to teach us the Father, the Son, and the holy Spirit at one and the same time, and included in his statement the incarnation of our lord, which took place for our salvation; through it the divine nature became our savior. With the words "The lord, through whom everything is, is one" (I Cor. 8.6), therefore, he teaches us about God the Word, who is a true Son, of the same nature as his Father, and he correctly names him lord, to make us understand that he is of the divine nature of God the Father.

The Father, then, was not called "one God," in order to deny that the Son was God, nor was the Son called "one lord," in the sense that the Father was not lord. It is quite clear and obvious that one who is truly God is also truly lord, just as one who is truly lord is also truly God. Whoever is not truly God is also not truly lord, since "the lord your God alone is lord" (Dt. 6.4), since he alone truly exists. The one who truly has both of these qualities is the only one who was truly called lord and God, and there is nothing, apart from this nature, that is called lord and God.

3. The person who says "one God," therefore, also shows

that the lord is one; and whoever says that the lord is one, confesses too that God is one. That is why [Paul said] in the earlier quote that "God is one," and then that "the lord is one"—he was distinguishing the individuals. He affirms of each individual that it is "one," so that the two individuals might be known to be one divine nature, which is truly lord and God.

4. Furthermore, to include in their words the human nature assumed for our salvation, the fathers at Nicaea said, "one lord, Jesus Christ," because that is the name of the human being with whom God was clothed, according to the word of the angel, "She will beget a son, and he will be called by the name of Jesus" (Lk. 1.31). But they also added "Christ," in order to make the holy Spirit known: "Jesus the Nazarene, whom God anointed with the holy Spirit and with power" (Acts 10.38). He is God because of the perfect joining with this divine nature, which is truly God. Our blessed fathers, who were united in this glorious synod of the universal church, also imitated Paul, by speaking first of the divine nature, and then by adding a word which indicates the human form that he took: "and in one lord Jesus Christ, only Son of God, firstborn of all creatures." In this way they wished to instruct people, by making the Son's divine nature known, while at the same time confessing his humanity, in which the divine nature was known and proclaimed, as saint Paul said, "God was seen in the flesh" (I Tim. 3.16). In the same vein, John the evangelist said, "The Word became flesh and dwelt among us, and we have seen his glory, like the glory of the only Son, sprung from the Father, full of grace and truth" (Jn. 1.14). Our fathers were quite right, then, to think that they should not neglect the teaching about our lord's humanity, which is associated in an indescribable way with the divine nature.

5. "And in one lord Jesus Christ." We confess, they say, that there is one lord who is of the divine nature, to whom these names of lord and God really belong. They make God the Word known to us with the words, "by whom everything was made," just as the evangelist said, "by him everything

was made, and without him nothing was made" (John 1.3).
It is he, they say, whom we hold to be the one lord, who is of
the divine nature of God the Father (that nature which for us
was clothed with a human being, lived in him, and was
revealed by him and known by all people), for he is that
human person of whom the angel said that he would be
called Jesus. And he was anointed by the holy Spirit, by
whom he was made perfect and justified, according to the
testimony of saint Paul.

6. After having taught in these words both the divine
nature and the human nature with which God was clothed,
[our fathers] then added, "only Son, firstborn of all creatures." With two words, they informed us of the two
natures,[8] and through the difference of the names they
taught us the distinction of the natures. Those who predicated these two realities of the single person of the Son,
showed us the extent to which the two natures were joined.
It was not of themselves that they used such terms, but
because of the teaching of the holy books, for Paul said, "It
is from them [i.e., the Israelites] that Christ sprang according
to the flesh, God above all" (Rom. 9.5). It is not that the one
who sprang from the house of David according to the flesh is
God by nature; he said "according to the flesh" to denote the
assumed human nature, while "God above all" is to teach us
about the divine nature, raised above everything, which is
the lord.

7. These two terms were predicated of the one person at
one and the same time, in order to teach the exact joining of
the two natures, and to make known the majesty of the
divinity possessed by the assumed human being with whom
God is clothed. It was of this same form that they said, "only
Son, firstborn of all creatures." On the subject of the two
natures, therefore, they had to teach us how they exist,
which is the divine nature that lowered itself, and which is
the assumed human nature; for this reason they first of all

[8]The Greek for "only Son, firstborn" consists of two words.

pronounced at one time these two names, by which they denoted the two natures. It is evident, then, that it is not one single nature which they call "only and firstborn of all creatures," since one cannot predicate these two things of one nature. There is, in fact, a great difference between an only son and a firstborn son, and it is impossible for the same person to be both only and firstborn. For "firstborn" is used when there are many brothers, while "only" is the one who does not have a brother. The difference between an only son and a firstborn son is the same as the one between the nature which is one and that which is common to many. He is called "only" who has absolutely no brothers, while he obviously is called "firstborn" who has brothers.

8. That is precisely what sacred scripture teaches us, for, when it wanted to speak about the only Son, it said, "We have seen his glory as the glory of an only Son sprung from the father" (John 1.14). It also said, "The only son, who is in the bosom of his father" (John 1.18), so that the only Son might be known through his connection with his Father. "We have seen his glory as the glory of an only son sprung from the father" shows that he alone exists by generation from the Father's nature, and that he alone is the Son. With the word "bosom," then, he teaches the inseparable joining that exists from all eternity; for it would be shameful to conceive of a corporeal bosom in God. Just as scripture, therefore, refers to vision as an eye and to hearing as an ear, so it calls the eternally inseparable joining a bosom, as in the phrase, "Pay seven for one into the neighbors' bosoms" (Ps. 79.12 [LXX,78.12]), which means, let them receive punishment continually and always. The meaning of the words "the only Son" is, then, this: he who alone exists through generation from the Father is alone Son, always exists with his Father and is known with him, because he is truly the Son sprung from his Father.

9. As for "firstborn of all creatures," let us understand it as we do the saying, "Those whom he foreknew he chose and marked out in the likeness of the image of his son, so that he might become the firstborn among many brothers" (Rom.

8.29). He used the word "firstborn," not to teach us that he is an only son, but to make us understand that he has many brothers. For it is known that innumerable are those who share with him in filial adoption, and because of them he receives the name "firstborn," since they are his brothers.

The same words appear elsewhere as well: "Firstborn of all creatures" (Col. 1.15) was said about Christ's incarnation. He did not, then, simply call him "firstborn," but added "of all creatures," since one is not called "firstborn," if one does not have brothers, because of whom one is called and is firstborn. He was also called "firstborn of all creatures," because, through the resurrection from the dead, he was the first one who was renewed and transformed into a wonderful new life; and so he renewed all creatures and led them to a glorious restoration. "For," it is said, "everything which is in Christ is a new creature; old things have passed away, and all has been renewed in our lord Jesus Christ" (II Cor. 5.17). He is, therefore, "firstborn of all creatures," because all creation has been renewed and transformed in this renewal, which, through grace, he has given to it; and this took place through the renewal which he first of all received, when he passed to a new life and was raised above all creatures. And so he was rightly called "firstborn of all creatures," because he himself had been first of all renewed, and had finally renewed creatures, since he had been raised higher than all of them in dignity.

10. Here is how we understand the difference between the two words: our fathers understood this difference as referring to one person, when, taught by the holy books, they said, "in one Son, the only Son, firstborn of all creatures." They said this to show us, as I have already said, the exact joining of the two natures. It was quite correct, therefore, for them to have said first "only," and then "firstborn," for it was right for them to have shown us first who it is who is in the form of God and who mercifully assumed [one] of our nature, and then to have spoken to us about the form of a slave that was assumed for our salvation (see Phil. 2.6-7). In this way they made us aware, through the different words

they used, of the two natures and their differences, and of the fact that the Son is an only Son because of the exact joining of the natures brought about by the divine will.

Keeping the order which is imposed by reality, they taught first about the divine nature, which through mercy lowered itself to us and clothed itself with a human being, and then about that very humanity which was assumed through grace; finally, as solid teaching to confound the heretics who struggle in opposition to the truth, they set themselves in their teaching to speak of the divine nature, about which they had spoken in the beginning of the profession of faith: "who was begotten by the Father before all ages and was not made."

11. It is obvious that they said this in reference to the divine nature, although, for people who are not argumentative, the word "only" would have been enough to teach them an exact knowledge of the Son; for if he is an only son, it is certain that he alone is generated from the Father and that he alone is Son, of the same nature as his Father. All this, then, is what the name "only Son" signifies, and all the more so because many are called sons of God, while he alone is the only Son. It was written, "I have said, 'You are gods and all sons of the most high;'" (Ps. 82.6 [LXX, 81.6]) and again, "I have nourished sons and have raised them" (Is. 1.2). Since there are so many who are named sons, he would not have been called "only son," if there had not been a great difference among them.

They are called sons through grace, because they became close and developed a relationship; because of this relationship they obtained, through grace, the favor of carrying this name. But as for him, he was called "only Son," because he alone is Son, of the nature of his Father. It was not as with the others, through grace, that he earned filial adoption and received for it the name of son; he was called, and is Son, because he was begotten of the same nature. And even though this is known and revealed in holy scripture, and even though it is obvious to everyone that one cannot be called an only son, if one is not the only one who is truly a son of his father's nature, still the evil and stubborn opinion of the heretics remains incorrigible.

12. Of all those who came to know Christ, then, Arius was the first one who had the wicked audacity to say that the Son is a work [of God] and made of nothing; this was something new, foreign to the usual way of seeing things and to the laws of nature. For what is made is not a son, and a son is not a creature, because it is impossible for a work to be called a son, just as it is impossible for a true son to be called a work. For this reason, then, our holy fathers had to gather together from all directions to form a holy synod in the city of Nicaea in the region of Bithynia; and they wrote this profession of faith to preserve the teaching of the truth, to suppress the wickedness of Arius, to refute those who would arise later under the name of their seducer Eunomius, and to destroy the heresies composed of evil beliefs.

13. They also added the following words, even though their content was absolutely obvious to everybody from the natural law, general agreement, and the teaching of the holy books: "who was begotten and not made." They proposed, therefore, words which suited the confession of faith in the Son, because, they said, we mean a son, not in an ordinary way, nor as one for whom it is an assumed name, as it is for those who receive the name of son through grace because of their relationship—we mean a true son and him alone. He is a true son because he is the one and only one begotten by his father and sprung from him.

It is part of his nature and of reality for him to be begotten and to exist from all eternity like the Father. No created being exists before the ages, but he does exist before the ages, who alone exists from all eternity. Just as the Father exists from all eternity, so does the Son who sprang from him exist from all eternity. He did not come into being after a period of time, nor was he begotten later on; from all eternity, before all the ages, he was begotten by that one who exists from all eternity, and he exists with him from all eternity. The evangelist says, "In the beginning was the Word" (Jn. 1.1). He exists from all eternity, and it was not at a later period that he came into being; before everything, "in the beginning," he was. In other words, he existed from all eternity, before all the ages, with God.

Fifth Catechetical Homily[9]

1. I know that you remember what we said to you about the divinity of the only Son, and how our blessed fathers, after teaching about the Father, approched also the words spoken about the Son in the holy books, and presented together the divinity of the Son and the form of a human which he took for our salvation. They felt that they should not pass over in silence the human nature with which he clothed himself, since it is through it that we obtained knowledge of the divine nature of the only Son. After saying "in one lord Jesus Christ," therefore, in order to reveal to us the divine nature and the human nature, they added, "the only Son, firstborn of all creatures," and preached to us once more the divine nature and the form of a human which was assumed for our salvation.

In order to teach us everything gradually and with precision—first of all about the only Son's divinity and about the way in which we believe that it exists—they handed the tradition on to us in the following words: the only Son, who is of the Father's nature, is not a son by an assumed name, as are other human beings who are sons by grace and not by nature; he is a true Son, born of the Father. For this reason he is also the only Son, since he alone is born of the nature of his Father. It is not that he became a son or received that name; from the beginning, before all ages, born of his Father, he exists from all eternity and was not made. The Son of God must not be called a work of God, therefore, since he did not come into existence from nothing, in accordance with the law of all creatures, but exists from all eternity "from his Father, true God from true God, of one nature with his Father," since he is a true Son and is by nature exactly the same as the one who begets him.

2. That is the precise teaching of our fathers on the divinity of the only Son, and such is the profession of faith which they set firmly in our souls, casting far away from us the opinion of the wicked people who dare to say that the Son of God was made or created—the Son who from all eternity,

[9]Text: Tonneau, 99-131.

before all ages, was born of his Father. After cleansing our minds of all heretical deceit, they began to speak also about the Incarnation of our lord, which took place for our salvation; they said, "who, for us humans and for our salvation, came down from heaven, was made flesh, and became human."

3. They were quite right to start with the phrase "for us humans and for our salvation," because they were going to speak about the divine plan based on his humanity and to explain first the reason for it; now they could not do that through those words about the only Son's divinity, [since they were concerned there] to show us how he existed from his Father from all eternity. When they set themselves to instruct us about his humanity, however, before all else they had to tell us why the divine nature lowered itself in this way: "for us," therefore, and because it was concerned for "our salvation," it assumed the form of a slave (see Phil. 2.7).

In beginning to teach about the divine plan based on his humanity, therefore, our fathers had to put as the starting-point of their discourse this reason: "who, for us humans and for our salvation." The phrase "for our salvation" is properly placed after the words "for us humans." It was not only "for humans"; but the actual reason for his coming, about which they are teaching us, was that he came to save humans, so that he might, by unspeakable grace and mercy, give life to, and free from evil those who had been lost and handed over to evil. This is why, according to them, he descended from heaven.

4. Consider now the words "he descended"; this did not happen by his moving from one place to another. For we must not think that the divine nature, which is everywhere, moves from one place to another, since it is not even possible for the divine nature, which is incorporeal, to be enclosed in one place; but what is not enclosed in one place is every-where, and it is impossible to imagine something which is everywhere moving from one place to another.

John testifies to this when he says, "He was in the world, and the world was made by him, and the world did not know him. He came to his own, and his own did not receive him" (John 1.10-11). Notice that he says that he was in the world and that he came into the world. If he was in the world, how could he come into it? For how can you say that one comes to a place where one already was? He says that "he was in the world" to show that he is everywhere; and he added "he came to his own," with reference to the divine plan based on the humanity. This is why David also said, "He lowered the heavens and came down" (Ps. 18.9 [LXX, 17.10]); he wanted to teach us that God saved them from their troubles. What he calls "God's descent" is God's condescension;[10] the one who was raised so high above everything else condescended to save them from trouble.

In the same way, the divine Word, the only son of God, is also said to have come down for our salvation, because he exists from his Father from all eternity and with him for all time, raised above everything; although he is the cause of everything, he nonetheless willingly took upon himself to come down to such a humiliation as to take the form of a slave (see Phil. 2.7) and to come into existence in it, so as to give us, through it, the enjoyment of his wondrous gift.

5. Our blessed fathers were right, then, to say, "for us humans and for our salvation he came down from heaven." What they call descent of the most high is the divine plan based on his humanity, at which even holy David was amazed: "What is a human being," he said, "that you remember it, and the son of man that you have visited him?" (Ps. 8.4 [LXX, 8.5])

"Who, for us humans and for our salvation, came down from heaven." What is the meaning of his descent, therefore, and what is its goal? And what does humanity become, so that, for it, the only Son lowered himself to the point of becoming human and of taking the form of a slave? For our

---

[10]"Condescension" and "condescend" do not have the negative meaning of the common English usage here; they signify God's gracious kindness in deigning to deal with humanity on its own level, and involve a play on the meaning of "condescension" in a spatial sense, as a "coming down."

salvation he was willing to become human and to show himself to all. He took upon himself all that belongs to the nature of the human being. Tested in all his faculties, he perfected the human by his power, to the extent that, even when it underwent death according to the law of its nature, he did not distance himself from the human, but, staying with it, snatched it, by the working of grace, from death and the corruption of the tomb, raised it from the dead, and gave it that high honor which he had promised it before undergoing death, when he said, "Destroy this temple, and in three days I shall raise it up again" (Jn. 2.19); and that is what he did.

6. He did not separate himself from the human when he was crucified, nor did he distance himself from it in death. He remained until the time when, with the help of his power, he broke the chains of death and freed his soul from the bonds that could not be broken; he raised the human from the dead and transferred it to a life untouched by death; he made it immortal, incorruptible, and immutable, and made it rise up to heaven, where now, according to the testimony of Paul, it "is seated at the right hand of God and is above every rule, authority, power, and dominion, and above every name which is named, not only in this world, but also in the one to come" (Eph. 1.20-21); the human receives adoration continually from all creation because of its very close union with God the Word.

7. Our fathers, therefore, had every right to say "who was made flesh and became human" about the one who, for our salvation, carried out such a plan as to be thought an ordinary human being by those who did not recognize the divinity living in him, but whose whole attention was directed to the visible. "The Jews," in fact, "said to him, 'It is not for good works that we stone you, but because you blaspheme, since, being human, you make yourself God'" (Jn. 10.33). Paul too says that he was human; "He was," he says, "in the likeness of humans, and it is in the form of a human that he is found" (Phil. 2.7). "Form of a human" means simply that he became human. For when scripture says "God sent his

Son, and he appeared in the likeness of the flesh of sin" (Rom. 8.3), "the likeness of the flesh" means the flesh itself, just as the scripture says elsewhere, "he appeared in the flesh" (I Tim. 3.16). Since it said "flesh" in the latter quote and "likeness of the flesh" in the former one, the word "flesh" says exactly the same to us as the words "likeness of the flesh"; so scripture teaches twice that he appeared in the flesh.

In the same way, this word "form" has no other meaning than "human." Rightly, then, did our blessed fathers say, "who was made flesh and became human," to show that he became human, as Paul testifies, and that it is for the salvation of all that he carried out this plan. It was absolutely correct, therefore, for our blessed fathers, in stating the faith, to have used this phrase to annihilate heretical wickedness, since they were in total accord with the profession of the true faith of the church. And because there were countless divisions among people on the topic of this ineffable plan and on the subject of the human which our lord assumed, to destroy all of these they were right to use the phrase, "who was made flesh and became human."

8. The followers of Marcion, the Manichaeans, the Valentinians, and the other heretics who suffer from this disease, all say that our lord took neither of our natures, body or soul, but that it was a phantom which appeared to human eyes, much like the vision which the prophets had (see Is. 6.1 ff. and Ezek. 1.1), or like the form in which Abraham saw three men, none of whom possessed a bodily nature, although they were throught to be men and performed human activities, such as walking, speaking, washing, eating, and drinking (see Gen. 18.1 ff.). In this way also, they said, our lord assumed nothing bodily; people believed him to be human because they saw him doing and undergoing everything in accordance with the laws of human nature. What was visible, however, was not the human nature, but merely a vision of it; it was thought to be the human nature, but in reality it underwent nothing, although those who saw it thought that it did.

9. The disciples of Arius and Eunomius said that he took a body, but not a soul; the divine nature, they said, replaced the soul. And they degrade the only Son's divine nature so far as to say that he falls from his natural greatness and performs the soul's activities, enclosing himself in this body and doing everything to keep it in existence. But if the divinity takes the place of the soul, then he was not hungry or thirsty, did not grow weary, and needed no nourishment, since all of this happens to the body because of its weakness, and because the soul can only supply the body's needs from what it has in accordance with the law of the nature that God gave it. But the soul needs a body perfect in everything, if it is to make the body exist; if something is lacking to the body, not only can the soul not help it in anyway at all, but the soul is overcome by the body's weakness and is forced, against its will, to leave it. But if the divinity had fulfilled the soul's function, then it would of necessity have performed the body's role as well, and it would seem that the teaching of those mad heretics was true, although they deny that the Son had taken a body, and said that it is only in a kind of form that one sees him, just as with the angels: they teach that he was only human in appearance, since he in no way possessed human nature.

The divinity was, of course, capable of fulfilling the function of everything and of causing spectators to believe that they saw "as though a human"; this is how, because of God's will, Abraham saw the angels. But if his divine nature sufficed for all of this, then it was not necessary for him, was it, to take on the human nature, which needed the grace of the salvation that comes from God? And if, as the heretics say, the divinity itself performed the role of the human nature, then there was no reason to assume a body, since the divinity could have done everything.

10. But this was not what God wanted; God wished to be clothed with, and to raise up again the human that had fallen, the human composed of a body and a soul that is both immortal and rational, so that, "just as through one person sin entered the world, and through sin death, so also

the grace and the gift of God, through the righteousness of a single person, Jesus Christ, are so much the greater" (Rom. 5.12 and 15); and Paul's testimony also says, "since death came through one person, so too resurrection from the dead comes through one person. As we all die through Adam, so we all live through Christ" (I Cor. 15.21-22).

It was not, then, simply a body that the Son had to assume, but a soul as well, and one that was immortal and rational. And it was not merely the death of the body that he had to destroy, but that of the soul, which is sin. For, since "sin entered the world through one person," as St. Paul says, "and death has now made its entry through sin" (Rom. 5.12), the sin that caused death had to be removed first, and then death would be destroyed along with it. But if sin is not removed, then we are doomed to live in mortality, and in our mutability we sin; and if we sin, we will again be subject to punishment and the power of death will again inevitably endure.

11. It was right, therefore, that, before anything else, sin had to be destroyed, because after the destruction of sin there was no longer any way for death to enter. Now it is clear that the inclination to sin begins in the soul's will, because, even in Adam, it was first of all the soul, not his body, which listened to the advice to stray; for it was not his body that Satan persuaded, through lust for noble goods, to yield to him, to withdraw from God, and to consider a seducer the one who would have helped him. Adam broke God's commandment, and, following Satan's advice, preferred what was contrary to God's commandment. It was not his body which should have understood these things, but his soul, which lusted for the promised greatness; it is the soul which welcomed the advice of the crafty one and which caused him to lose the goods that it had.

It is not only a body, therefore, that the Christ had to assume, but a soul as well; indeed, the soul had to be assumed first of all, and then, because of it, the body. For if death comes from sin and is the corruption of the body, then sin must be destroyed first, and then death must be annihilated along with it; in this way, the body would be freed from death and corruption. Now this was possible if Christ first of all made the soul immutable and delivered it from the movements of sin, for in acquiring immutability we would be freed from sin. The destruction of sin causes the destruction of death, and by the fact that death is destroyed, our body can be indissoluble and incorruptible.

12. If the soul committed only those sins which stem from the body's passions, it would then perhaps have sufficed for our lord to take only a body in order to save the soul from sin; but as things stand, the soul itself gives rise to the numerous and shameful evils of sin, and especially that one which makes it clear that the soul is in partnership with Satan, namely, pride, of which St. Paul said, "out of fear that he become puffed up with pride and fall under the same judgement as Satan" (I Tim. 3.6). By saying this the apostle showed that anyone who falls into pride is in fellowship with Satan in the matter of punishment, because such a one has received in his soul that passion which Satan, although bodiless, possesses by the wickedness of his knowledge; it is quite certain, then, that the soul requires a great deal of care to be freed from falling and to be saved also from the body's passions which, through the power the body has, can dominate the soul.

13. Paul witnesses to our interpretation in his enumeration of the evils toward which the people whom the Christ came into the world to cure are drawn, and to which they lower themselves; he said, "Because of this, God delivered them to their evil sense, so that they do what they should not do, filled with every type of sin, iniquity, and evil, such as avarice, fornication, bitterness, envy, murder, fighting, robbery, wickedness, and calumny; hating God, they are filthy people, proud, boastful, clever at devising evil, rebellious against their parents, possessing neither fidelity nor mercy" (Rom. 1.28-31). Everyone, even before we spoke, knows this with certitude and is aware that many of these things are the product, not of the body's faculties, but of the soul's will and that alone.

14. Our lord had to take a soul, then, so that it might first be saved from sin and move on through God's grace to immutability, by which the soul also controls the body's passions. When sin has finally been abolished and can no longer enter into the soul, which has become immutable, then every form of punishment is of necessity also abolished, and death too is destroyed. And so it is that the body will live on, having become a stranger to death, because it participates in immortality. This is what Paul affirms when he says, "Henceforth there is no more condemnation among those who, in Christ Jesus, no longer act according to the flesh; because the law of the spirit of life in Chirst Jesus has made you free with respect to the law" (Rom. 8.1-2). He is saying that every sentence of death and every condemnation were abolished for those who believed in Christ, because they became strangers to the ways of mortality, received the Spirit and immortality, obtained immutablity along with them, and have been completely freed from sin and mortality.

15. It is, then, a sign of total insanity not to acknowledge that the Christ took a soul; furthermore anyone who says that he did not take a human intellect is also quite mad, since such a person is saying, either that he assumed no soul at all, or that he assumed a soul, but that it was a non-human, non-intelligent one, of the type that gives life to dumb animals. The human soul differs from that of the animals in this alone, that the latter soul does not have an individual existence on its own; in the composition of the animal, the soul does not exist by itself apart from the existence of the whole animal, and after the death of the animal, the belief is that the soul no longer exists. Thus the blood of the animals is said to be their soul, since at the same time that the blood is shed, there perishes also what is called the soul, which, before the animal's death, was thought to exist in their individual existence as a whole and in their faculties.

But it is different with humans. The soul has an individual existence of its own and is raised high above the body, since the body is mortal, and since it is from the soul that the body receives life; and the body dies and is dissolved, if it comes about that the soul leaves it. But the soul, even in going away, remains indestructible and lives forever in its own individual existence, for it is immortal and by nature can suffer nothing from human beings. "Do not fear," it was said, "those who kill the body, because they cannot kill the soul" (Mt. 10.28). Surely this statement teaches clearly that the body can die because it is mortal by nature, while the soul remains immortal, because it can suffer no harm from human activity.

16. The difference between the human soul and the animal soul is so great, then, that the latter lacks reason and does not have individual existence on its own, while the human soul is immortal and is, therefore, also thought to be of necessity intelligent. Who then would be so mad or so lacking in human intelligence as to say that the soul of a human being exists without understanding and reason? Only a person who desired to become a new teacher of something that does not exist anywhere: an immortal nature, which lives with a life that cannot perish, but which nevertheless lacks reason. This is, of course, impossible. In fact, whatever is immortal by its nature and possesses imperishable life is also, in reality, capable of knowing and is endowed with reason.

17. But our blessed fathers guarded against all this by saying, "who was made flesh and became human," so that we might believe that the one who was assumed and in whom God the Word dwelled was a perfect human—this one was perfect in everything belonging to human nature and existed in a state that resulted from a mortal body and a rational soul, because it is "for humans and for human salvation that he descended from heaven." It was correct, then, for them to say that he took a human being like those from whom he was taken; for the human whom he assumed was like Adam, who introduced sin into the world, and so he abolished sin through one who was of the same nature as Adam. And he clothed himself in a human like Adam, who, after having sinned, had been sentenced to death, so that through a similar being sin might be uprooted from among us and death might be abolished.

18. "The prince of this world comes," he said, " and has nothing in me" (Jn. 14.30); thus he reveals that this is the reason for his resurrection from the dead. Since Satan held the power of death because of the sin that was in us, according to what Paul said, death prevailed, and thus, as slaves of sin, we could hope for no deliverance; the grace of God, therefore, kept free from sin the human whom God put on for us. Satan rushed in and by deceit aroused all the Jews against him, and brought death on him as on a human. Since he had no form of sin which would subject our lord the Christ to death, the latter took upon himself the death which, through wickedness, the tyrant Satan brought on him (see Rom. 3-8).

But the Christ showed God that he had no sin and that it was unjust for him to undergo the test of death, and he easily obtained the abolition of the punishment; he rose from the dead through the divine power, deservedly won eternal and ineffable life, and gave this universal grace to the whole human race. That is why our lord said here, "The prince of this world comes and has nothing in me" (Jn. 14.30), while elsewhere he said, "Now is the judgement of this world; now the prince of this world has been condemned and cast out. And I, when I have been raised from the earth, shall draw all to me" (Jn. 12.31-32). Through the first text he shows that Satan had no just cause to inflict death on him; in the second text, he says that he could, as it were, judge the tyrant, that he condemned him and drove him from his evil power, and then, since he himself was in command of these wonderful benefits, he gave all humans a share in his glory.

19. And so our blessed fathers said, "who was made flesh," so that you could understand that it was a perfect human that he took; it was not for his appearance alone that he was thought to be such, but because he truly had human nature. And, it is believed, he took not only a body, but the whole human, composed of a body and an immortal and rational soul. He assumed it for our salvation, and through it he brought about salvation for our life. This human was made righteous and spotless through the power of the holy Spirit,

as Paul said: " He was made righteous by the Spirit" (I Tim. 3.16); St. Paul also said, "who in the eternal Spirit offered himself, spotless, to God" (Heb. 9.14).

After he underwent death in accordance with the law of humanity, he arose from the dead through the power of the Holy Spirit, because he was sinless, and he earned the new life in which the soul's acts of will are unchangeable. He rendered his body immortal and incorruptible, and thus made us all sharers in his promises. As a pledge of his promises, he gave us the firstfruits of the Spirit, so that we might believe without hesitation in the things to come. "He it is who has confirmed us with you in Christ and has marked us with his seal, and has given us the pledge of his Spirit in our hearts" (II Cor. 1.21-22).

20. We too are waiting, therefore, to become immortal and incorruptible at the resurrection from the dead, when sin will no longer be able to touch us. This is what Paul witnesses to when he says, "For it will come about that the corruptible will be clothed with incorruptibility, and the mortal with immortality; and when the corruptible is clothed with incorruptibility, and the mortal with immortality, then the word of scripture will be fulfilled; 'Death has been swallowed up in victory. Death, where is your victory? Death, where is your sting?' For the sting of death is sin, and the power of sin is the law" (I Cor. 15.53-56). He is saying that, when we are raised from the dead, immortal and incorruptible, and our nature has received immutability, then we will no longer be able to sin, and when we have been freed from sin, we will no longer need the law. For what need of law will a nature have that is freed from sin and is no longer capable of deviating toward evil?

21. It was good, then, that right after this, St. Paul said, "He gave us the victory through our lord Jesus Christ" (I Cor. 15.57), for he teaches us that it is God who caused every good for us, and who gave us the victory over all that is contrary to good, be it death, sin, or any other evil that happens. It is God who, for us, was clothed with our lord Jesus Christ, a human, and through the resurrection from

the dead made him pass to a new life and sit at God's right hand; and to us, through God's grace, God will give companionship with him, when, in truth, according to the words of Paul, "the body of our lowliness will be changed and will become the likeness of his glory" (Phil. 3.21).

Sixth Catechetical Homily[11]

1. Let us approach today, with the help of divine grace, the next words in the creed. After saying, "who, for us humans and for our salvation, came down from heaven, was made flesh, and became human," our fathers added, "who was born of the virgin Mary and was crucified in the time of Pontius Pilate." They could have mentioned many things that he did in between, as for example, that "he was wrapped in swaddling clothes and placed in a manger" (Lk. 2.7), that "he was subjected to the law" (Gal. 4.4), that "he presented himself for baptism" (Mt. 3.3.), or that he gave the example of an evangelical life (see Acts 1.1); they could have said many things like this, if they had wanted to relate everything that the sacred books contain about him.

2. He did all this for our salvation. He observed the law of nature perfectly for us, because he was going to reform our nature. He also observed the law of Moses perfectly, in order to pay for us the debt owed to the lawgiver. He offered himself for baptism, in order to provide a model for the grace of our baptism. In himself he provided everybody with an absolutely perfect example of the evangelical life. And after all that, he handed himself over to crucifixion and death, in order to "destroy the final enemy, which is death" (I Cor. 15.26), and to display clearly the new, immortal life.

But our fathers were careful to say everything briefly, so that their audience could understand them easily. They used few words in composing the creed, and so they said, "He who was born of the virgin Mary and was crucified in the time of Pontius Pilate." They mentioned the beginning and

[11]Text: Tonneau, 131-137.

the end of the plan of salvation [which was carried out] on our behalf; for the beginning of all grace was his birth from Mary, and the end was the crucifixion. For they call "cross" the passion and all that happened in the passion; everything was included in a single word, because through the cross came death, and then from death came immortal life. Thus St. Paul said, "The teaching of the cross is folly to unbelievers, but for us who have been saved it is the power of God" (I Cor. 1.18); and he also says, "surely he had been crucified in weakness, but he is living through the power of God" (II Cor. 13.4). He taught us that the doctrine of the cross is a power of God for those who live, because through it he abolished death and gave the example of a new life.

3. It is certain that it was not the divine nature of the only Son that they think was born of a woman, as though that nature had its beginning from that source; for that nature, of which they say "who was begotten from his Father before all ages and who from all eternity is from him and exists with him," did not have its beginning from Mary. But they followed the sacred books, which speak differently about the natures, teaching one single person because of the complete union which existed, and because of the fear that people might think that they were dividing the perfect union shared by that which was assumed and that which did the assuming. For if this union is abolished, that which was assumed no longer seems to be anything but a mere human being like ourselves. That is why the holy books proclaim the two terms as of a single Son—to reveal, in the profession of faith itself, the glory of the one and only Son, as well as the honor of the human with whom the Son was clothed.

4. After Paul said, "The Jews from whom the Christ comes," he added, "according to the flesh" (Rom. 9.5), in order to distinguish the natures. And he shows us that, when it is a question of the Christ who comes from the Jews according to the flesh, he does not think that it is the nature of the only begotten one's divinity, nor is it God the Word, of whom he says this. He is speaking about the form of a human that God the Word assumed.

2. CYRIL OF ALEXANDRIA

On the Gospel of John

1. *"Those who were born, not of blood, nor of the will of flesh, nor of the will of a man, but of God"* (Jn. 1.13).

Those people, he says, who were called through faith in Christ to be adopted children of God, have put off the defilement of their own nature, have been glorified, as by a splendid garment, through the grace of the one who honors them, and rise to supernatural dignity. For they are no longer called children of flesh, but rather adopted offspring of God. Notice how carefully the blessed evangelist chose his words. Since he was going to say that believers were begotten from God, he carefully works out an explanation, which we needed, so that no one would think that they were truly born from the substance of the one who is God and Father and that they, therefore, shared absolute similarity with the only begotten one; he also wanted to keep people from thinking that the words "I begot you from the womb before the daystar" (Ps. 110.3 [LXX, 109.3]) were spoken inexactly about the only begotten one, so that he would be brought down to the level of created natures, even though he is said to have been begotten by God. For after he had said that the natural Son had given them power to become children of God, and had indicated also that this would be through adoption and grace, he avoided danger by immediately adding the words, "They were born from God." He said this to display the richness of the grace they received, as God the Father gathers together into God's own nature those who are alien to God, and as the servant rises to the master's nobility because of the master's intense love for the servant.

Those who through faith in Christ rise up to adoption as children of God are baptized, through the mediation of the Word, not into a creature, but into the holy trinity itself; the Word does this by joining humanity to itself through the flesh united to it, and is itself united by nature to the one who begot it, since it is by nature God. The servant thus achieves childhood, through participation in the real Son, being called and, as it were, being raised up to the dignity he possesses by nature. We are, therefore, called, and actually are children of God, since through faith we were reborn through the Spirit.[12]

2. *"And the Word became flesh"* (Jn. 1.14).

With this phrase the evangelist has obviously moved to a discussion of [the Word's] becoming human. He explains clearly that the only begotten became and was called a son of man; for saying that "the Word became flesh" means that and nothing else. It is exactly the same as if he had said quite simply, "the Word became a human being." Using the part for the whole, he refers to the human being by saying flesh; he had to speak in this way, and it seems necessary to explain why. The human being is a rational, living being, composed of a soul and of this perishable, earthly flesh. When God made it and brought it into being, it was not of its own nature incorruptible and immortal, for these properties belonged by nature to God alone; it was sealed with the spirit of life, enjoying, through its relationship with God, goods that were far beyond its nature. But when it was punished for sin, it heard the just sentence, "You are earth and to earth you will return" (Gen. 3.19), and it was stripped of grace. The Spirit of life, that is, the Spirit that says, "I am the life" (Jn. 14.6), left the earthly flesh, and the living being is subjected to death through the flesh alone, since the soul continues to be immortal; for "You are earth and to earth you will return" was said to the flesh alone.

That part of us which was in the greatest danger had, therefore, to be saved as quickly as possible, and had to be recalled to immortality through union with a life in harmony with its nature. That which had suffered had to find a release from its troubles. The power of "you are earth and to earth

[12]Text: PG, 73.153-156.

you will return" had to be ended, and it was, when the body which had fallen was united in a marvellous way to the Word that gives life to everything. For the flesh, after becoming the Word's, had to share in the Word's immortality. And it would be very strange to think that the Word of God, which surpasses all things, could not implant in the flesh its own special good, which is life.

This, I think, is the main reason why the holy evangelist, referring to the living being through the part that had suffered, says that God's "Word became flesh"; he did it, so that, at one and the same time, one could see both the wound and the medicine, the one who is sick and the physician, the one inclined toward death and the one who raises to life, the one conquered by corruption and the one who drives corruption away, the one overcome by death and the one who is greater than death, the one deprived of life and the one who bestows life. He does not say that the Word came into flesh, but that "the Word became flesh," so that you do not think that the Word's coming is through a relationship, as happens with the prophets and other holy people, but that you might understand that the Word truly became flesh, that is, a human being. The Word is, therefore, God by nature, in flesh and with flesh, perceived as having God's own nature and something else beyond that as well, and adored both in and with that nature, as the prophet Isaiah said, "Stately men will come over to you and will be your servants; bound in chains they will follow after you, and they will adore you and pray to you, because God is in you, and there is no God apart from you" (Is. 45.14). Note that they say that God is in him, and do not separate the flesh from the Word; they also affirm that there is no other God but him, uniting to the Word, as the Word's very own, that which the Word wore, namely, the temple that comes from the virgin. For Christ is one out of both realities.[13]

[13]Text: PG, 73.157-161.

3. *"And dwelt among us"* (Jn. 1.14).

After saying that God's "Word became flesh," so that no one, through sheer ignorance, would assume that the Word had left its own nature, had actually been transformed into flesh, and thus underwent a change, which is an impossibility, because the divine, by reason of its very nature, is above all change and alteration, the evangelist did an excellent thing by adding immediately the words, "and dwelt among us." Through them one sees that there are two realities in question, the one who dwells and that in which the dwelling takes place, and one would not think that the Word was changed into flesh, but rather dwelt in flesh through the use of its body, the temple that comes from the holy virgin. "For the whole fullness of the divinity dwelt in him bodily," as Paul says (Col. 2.9). In affirming that "the Word dwelt among us," he reveals to us this very profound mystery. All of us were in Christ, and the common person of humanity comes to life again in him. For the last Adam was so named because, through a common nature, he brought all to the wealth of happiness and glory, just as the first Adam had brought all to corruption and sorrow (see I Cor. 15.45-49).

The Word, therefore, dwelt in all through one, so that, when the one had been designated Son of God in power, that glory might spread to all humanity in accordance with the spirit of holiness (see Rom. 1.4); and so the words, "I have said, 'You are gods and all sons of the most high'" (Ps. 82.6), could be applied to us because of one who was one of us. Thus the servant is truly freed in Christ, on the one hand, by rising up to a mystical union with the one who wears the form of the servant (see Phil. 2.7), and in us, on the other hand, by our imitation of the one who has kinship with us through the flesh. If this were not so, why "does he take hold, not of the angels, but of Abraham's seed, so that he had to become like his brethren in all things" (see Heb. 2.16-17), and truly become human? Is it not clear to everyone that the Word came down to this servile state, not to gain something for itself, but to give itself to us, so that we might become rich through his poverty, by obtaining through our likeness to him that special good which is his, and that we might appear as gods and children of God through faith? For the one who is Son by nature and God "dwelt among us," and "we," therefore, "cry out through his Spirit, 'Abba, father'" (see Rom. 8.15). The Word dwells among all, in the one temple assumed for us and from us, so that, having all in himself, he might reconcile all to the Father in one body, as Paul says (see Eph. 2.16).[14]

Letter 45: To Succensus[15]

4. We have learned from sacred scripture and the holy fathers to confess one Son, Christ, and lord, the Word that comes from God the Father, begotten from the Father before the ages in a divine and ineffable way, but in the last times of this age the same one born for us, according to the flesh, from the holy virgin; and since she gave birth to God who became human and took flesh, we call her mother of God. There is, therefore, one son, one lord Jesus Christ, both before the taking of flesh and after it. For the Word of God the Father is not one Son, while the holy virgin's son is a second one; the one who existed before time is believed also to have been born from a woman according to the flesh, but not in such a way that the Word's divinity started to exist, or that its existence as an individual was called into being through the holy virgin—as I said, the Word that exists before time is said to have been born of her according to the flesh. For the Word's flesh belonged to the Word, just as our own bodies belong to each one of us. (4)

5. We say that the Word of God the Father, in an incomprehensible way that cannot be explained, joined to itself a body that was animated by an intellectual soul, and came forth from a woman as a human being, and that the Word

[14]Text: PG, 73.161-164.
[15]Text: ACO I.1.6, 152-156.

became like us, not through a change of nature, but rather through the good will of the divine plan. For the Word wished to become human without losing its natural existence as God; and even though it came down with our limitations and bore the form of the servant, it continued to abide in its divine transcendence and with the power proper to its nature. To the sacred flesh that has a rational soul in an indescribable way that surpasses understanding, we, therefore, unite the Word of God the Father, in a union that admits of no confusion, change, or transformation, and we confess one Son, Christ, and lord; we confess that the same one is both God and a human being, not two separate individuals, and that one and the same being both is and is thought to be this. (5-6)

6. Sometimes, therefore, he talks as a human being, in a way that is human and in keeping with the divine plan, while at other times he speaks as God, with a power that is worthy of God. Here is what we say: when we carefully analyze the character of God's plan according to the flesh and consider the mystery in detail, we see that the Word of God the Father became human and took flesh, but did not form that sacred body out of its own divine nature; it took it rather from a virgin, for how could the Word have become a human being, if it did not possess a human body? As I said, therefore, when we consider the way in which the Word became human, we see that two natures came together in a union that cannot be broken, but that also admits of no confusion or change. For the flesh is flesh and not divinity, even though it was God's flesh, just as the Word is God and not flesh, even though the Word made the flesh its own in accordance with the divine plan. (6)

7. When we see this, therefore, we are not wrong to say that what took place was the joining of two natures in a unity; but even after the natures were united, we do not divide them from one another, nor do we cut the one, indivisible person into two sons. We affirm one Son, and, as the fathers taught, one nature, of the Word, become flesh. And so, insofar as we have been able to understand and concep-

tualize the manner in which the only begotten one became human, we state that the two natures were united, and that the Word of God became human and took flesh as one Christ, Son, and lord. (6-7)

8. If it seems helpful, let us use as an example our own composition, according to which we are human beings. We are composed of a soul and a body, and we see two natures, one of the body, and another of the soul; but one human being is the result of the union of these two, and the fact that the one [person] is composed of two natures does not produce two human beings, but one human being, composed, as I said, of body and soul. For if we do away with the idea that the one and only Christ, who cannot be divided after the union, comes from two different natures, the enemies of correct opinion will say, "If the whole reality is one nature, how did he become human and what flesh did he make his own?" (7)

9. Now since I found in your letter a reflection of the idea that after the resurrection the sacred body of Christ our savior changed into the divine nature, so that the whole being was only divine, I thought that I should also speak to this. Paul, in explaining to us the reasons why the only begotten Son of God became human, writes:

> What the law could not do because it was weakened by the flesh, God [did], by sending his own Son in the likeness of the flesh of sin and for sin; he condemned sin in the flesh, so that the justice of the law might be fulfilled in us, who walk, not according to flesh, but according to the Spirit (Rom. 8.3-4).

He also said:

> For since the children shared in blood and flesh, he also shared equally in the same qualities, so that through death he might render impotent the one who held the power of death, namely, the devil, and might free those who, through fear of death, were subject to slavery for life. For he does not take

hold of the angels, but does take hold of Abraham's seed; he, therefore, had to become like his brothers in every way (Heb. 2.14-17). (8)

10. We say, then, that due to Adam's sin human nature suffers corruption and that our rational powers are dominated by fleshly pleasures and innate passions; in order to save us earthly creatures, therefore, God's Word had to become human, so that it could take and make its own human flesh, which had been subjected to corruption and was suffering from an excessive love of pleasure; in this way, since the Word is life and giver of life, it would do away with the corruption of the flesh and discipline its innate passions, especially those which lead to an excessive love of pleasure. For sin was thus to be destroyed through that flesh, and we think of Paul who called the innate passion in us law of sin (see Rom. 7.23 and 25). Since human flesh, therefore, became the flesh of the Word, it stopped being subject to sin, and since the one who made it and called it its own did not, as God, know sin, it also, as I have said, stopped suffering from an excessive love of pleasure. (9)

11. The only begotten Word of God did not perform this good work for itself, for it is what it is, forever; it obviously did it for us. For if we were made subject to the evils that resulted from Adam's sin, we shall certainly also share in the results of Christ's work, which are freedom from corruption and the death of sin. The Word, therefore, became a human being and did not assume a human being, as Nestorius thinks; in order to stir up faith in the fact that the Word became a human being, while remaining what it was, God by nature, he is said to have been hungry, to grow weary from a journey, to feel the need for sleep, and to experience distress, grief, and the other non-sinful human emotions. And then, in order to convince those who saw him that, in addition to being a human being, he is true God, he worked miracles, rebuking the seas, raising the dead, and performing other remarkable good works. He even endured the cross, so that, by suffering death in the flesh, not in the divine nature, he

could become the firstborn from the dead (see Col. 1.18), prepare for human nature the road to immortality, and show pity by despoiling the underworld of the souls that were trapped there. (9)

12. After the resurrection the very same body that had suffered continued to exist, even though it no longer had human weaknesses in it. We say that it is no longer subject to hunger, weariness, and other problems like these; we hold that it is now incorruptible, and not only that, but is also a source of life. For it is the body of life, that is, of the only begotten one, it has been made splendid with a glory that is most worthy of God, and it is perceived as God's body. Anyone, therefore, who would call this body divine, in the way that one would call the body of a human being human, would be speaking quite properly; I think that this is why Paul, who was so wise, said, "Even if we knew Christ according to the flesh, now we no longer know him so" (II Cor. 5.16). (10)

13. Since it was, as I said, a body that belonged to God, it surpassed all human bodies, for an earthly body cannot undergo a change into the divine nature; that is impossible, since we will reject divinity that is begotten or that takes into itself something that does not belong to it by nature. For it is just as absurd to say that the body was transformed into the divine nature, as it is to claim that the Word was transformed into the nature of the flesh. The second alternative is impossible, since the Word is unchangeable and immutable, while the first one is equally impossible, because no creature can change into the substance or nature of the divinity, and the flesh is a creature. We say that the body of Christ is divine, therefore, because it is God's body, is resplendent with ineffable glory, and is incorruptible, sacred, and life-giving. But not one of our holy predecessors thought or said that it was transformed into the divine nature; and we do not think this either. (10)

Scholia

14. Sin ruled over everybody because of Adam's transgression; the holy Spirit departed from humanity which fell into total evil due to this guilt; and humanity, through God's mercy, had to return to what it was in the beginning in order to be judged worthy of the Spirit; the only begotten Word of God became flesh, therefore, appeared to people on earth with an earthly body, and was free of sin, so that, through it and it alone, human nature could be rewarded with the power to boast of sinlessness, could enjoy the riches of the holy Spirit, and thus could be consecrated and formed anew into God's image. For in this way that grace comes to us which first seized hold of Christ our firstborn. The Word of God, who became human like us for our sake, is called Christ; as a human, that Word is anointed according to the flesh in the form of the servant, while the Word, as God, anoints through its own Spirit those who believe in it.[16]

15. Let us contemplate the manner in which God's plan of salvation through the flesh was executed, and let us examine the condition in which we were. Human nature had fallen into danger and was buried in the depths of evil; it had been condemned by the curse of death, was entangled in the nets of sin, wandered about and existed in darkness, did not know the God who was really and truly God, and served creation instead of the creator. How, then, was it to be freed from such terrible evils? It would be more fitting and quite proper to realize that, out of a desire to save what was lost by coming down to our level, the one through whom all things exist, the divine Word, came down into that which it was not, so that human nature could become that which it was not, and could become distinguished, through union with the Word, by the overwhelming majesty of God.

Human nature was raised to a level beyond its nature, or rather achieved a state that was incompatible with its

[16]Text: ACO, I.5.1, 219-220.

nature, becoming like the immutable God. The incorruptible had to take hold of the nature subject to corruption, in order to free it from corruption; the one who did not know sin had to take on the same form as those who were subject to sin, in order to put a stop to sin. For just as darkness ceases to exist where there is light, so too, when incorruptibility is at hand, must corruption absolutely disappear, and sin must lose its power, when the one who does not know sin claims as its own the one who is subject to sin.[17]

16. When we hear that the Word became flesh, let us understand by this a human being composed of a soul and a body. The Word who was God became a complete human being, by taking a body with a soul and a mind; by truly uniting this to itself, in a mysterious way, the Word was called a son of man.[18]

3. THEODORET OF CYRUS

On [Divine] Providence (Tenth Discourse)

1. Let us say a few words about our savior's becoming human, which is the greatest single proof of God's concern for human beings. [Nothing in all of creation] shows God's immeasurable goodness as much as the fact that the only begotten Son of God—the one who existed in the form of God (see Phil. 2.6), radiance of the glory and image of the reality (see Heb. 1.3), the one who was in the beginning, and was with God, and was God, and through whom all things were made (see Jn. 1.1-3)—took the form of the servant, came into being in human likeness, was found as a human in human form (see Phil. 2.7-8), "was seen on the earth and associated with humans" (see Bar. 3.37 [LXX, 3.38]), assumed our weaknesses, and bore our sicknesses. It is not, therefore, that God is simply concerned about

[17]Text: ACO, I.5.1, 227.
[18]Text: ACO, I.5.1, 228.

human beings; God loves them and for that reason is concerned about them.[19]

2. This divine love is so overwhelming that God declared that the only begotten Son (the consubstantial one, born from God's womb before the daystar, with whom God worked in forming creation) was our healer and savior, and granted us, through him, the gift of adoption. For the creator saw that human beings had gone over willingly to the cruel tyrant, that they had fallen into the very pit of evil, that they were trampling boldly on the laws of nature, and that visible creation, which spoke of and proclaimed the creator, could not win over these people who had sunk into ultimate insensibility; seeing all this, the creator worked out our salvation with wisdom and justice. For the creator did not wish to give us freedom through the use of force alone, nor to employ only mercy as a weapon against the one who enslaved human nature, lest the latter should call that mercy unjust; instead the creator devised a way that is filled with love for humanity and adorned with justice.[20]

3. The creator united the conquered nature to himself and leads it into battle, preparing it to undo that defeat, to fight against the one who had wickedly conquered it long ago, to destroy the power of the one who had shamefully enslaved it, and to recover its former freedom. The lord Christ is born of a woman, therefore, just as we are, although this birth contains another element, namely, virginity. For it was a virgin who conceived and bore the lord Christ. When you hear the word Christ, think of the only begotten Son, the Word, begotten of the Father before the ages, clothed in human nature; but do not imagine that this plan of God which we proclaim is contaminated in any way. For nothing can defile the pure nature [of God]. Let us, then, stand in awe before the one who did not entrust

[19]Text: PG, 83.745C-748A.
[20]Text: PG, 83.748BC.

our care to angels, but took upon himself the task of treating and curing human beings.[21]

4. This, then, is how the lord Christ was born: he sucks his mother's breast as we do; he is placed in a crib that served as a food-trough for animals, and thus censures human foolishness and displays his own love for humanity; for he provides nourishment as God, and in his humanity becomes the food of human beings, who were suffering from the terrible disease of foolishness. But now that human nature has cast off foolishness and taken on reason, it is welcomed at the mystical table, which is symbolized by the crib.[22]

5. The holy Spirit teaches through the prophet that he was wounded for our sins and was made weak because of our lawlessness. And this is clarified in the words, "Chastisement for our peace was upon him, and by his bruises we were healed" (Is. 53.5). For we were God's enemies, since we had offended, and, therefore, we deserved chastisement and punishment. But we did not experience this; instead our savior himself endured it, and by doing so he gave us peace with God. The next words make it even more clear: "We had all gone astray like sheep; humanity had gone astray from its path. He was, therefore, led like a sheep to slaughter, and was silent like a lamb before its shearer" (Is. 53.6-7). He found it right to cure like by like, and, through a sheep, to call the sheep back from their wandering. He becomes a sheep, but is not transformed into a sheep; nor does he undergo a change, or step out of his own nature. It is clear that he put on the nature of the sheep, and like the ram which leads the flock, he became ram of the flock and caused all the sheep to follow him. He was, therefore, like a sheep and a sacrificial victim, and was offered as a sacrifice for the whole race.[23]

[21]Text: PG, 83.748C-749C.

[22]Text: PG, 83.749CD.

[23]Text: PG, 83.756AB.

6. The prophet had a reason for mentioning the slaughter and the shearing together. Since he was both God and a human being, when the body was slaughtered, the divine nature remained untouched, and, therefore, Isaiah had to show us the slaughter of the sheep and the shearing of the lamb. For he was not only slaughtered, he says; he was also sheared. He suffered death in his humanity, but remained alive and untouched as God, and gave the wool of his body to the shearers. This is how Isaiah showed us the sufferings that gave salvation and how he taught the reasons for these sufferings.[24]

7. Paul says clearly, "Christ bought us from the curse of the law, having become a curse for us. For it was written, 'Cursed is everyone who is hung on a tree'" (Gal. 3.13). In saying "for us," he showed that Christ, who was free from guilt and completely innocent of sin, paid our debt, and also that he honored us with freedom, when we were crushed under countless debts and were for that reason forced into slavery; he did this by redeeming us, putting down his own blood as a price. Paul, therefore, says elsewhere, "We have been bought for a price" (I Cor. 6.20), and also, "Through your knowledge the weak brother, for whom Christ died, is destroyed" (I Cor. 8.11). This is why he endured death on a cross: that type of death was, according to the law, accursed, and accursed too was [human] nature, which had broken the law. For "cursed," it says, "is everyone who does not abide by the contents of the book of the law to observe them" (Dt. 27.6). He accepts the universal curse, therefore, and destroys it through the unjust slaughter. For he was not subject to the curse, since he did not commit sin, and no deceit was found in his mouth (see I Pt. 2.22 and Is. 53.9); still he underwent the death of sinners and sits in judgement on the destroyer, the enemy of all our nature, becoming both defender of, and pleader for our nature.[25]

24 Text: PG, 83.756BC.
25 Text: PG, 83.756C-757A.

8. Correctly, then, does he say to our bitter enemy, "You have been caught, evil one, in your own nets, your sword has pierced your own heart, and your arrows are broken. You have dug a trap and fallen into it yourself; the snares you have set have tied your own hands. Tell me, why did you nail my body to the cross and send me to death? What kind of sin did you see in me? What law did you see broken? Divine law handed sinners over to death, but you have put into the chains of death one who is innocent of sin. Your insatiable greed is the reason for your horrible cruelty; since you have taken one person unjustly, you have been stripped of all those who were rightly subject to you. You have eaten food that should not be eaten, and you will vomit up everything you have swallowed to this time. Since you, who received power over sinners, grasped a body which committed no sin, give up your power, lay aside your tyranny. I shall free all people from death, not through mercy alone, but through a just mercy, and not through the exercise of tyrannical power, but through just power. For I have paid the debt for the race."[26]

9. After saying this, the lord raised his own body and sowed the seeds of hope for the resurrection in human nature, giving the resurrection of his own body as a pledge to all.[27]

Letter 16: To Bishop Irenaeus

10. What difference does it make if we call the holy virgin "mother of a human being" as well as "mother of God," or if we say that she is mother and servant of the one she bore, adding that she is mother of our lord Jesus Christ insofar as he is human, and his servant insofar as he is God? In this way one does not provide a pretext for slander and expresses the same idea in a different word. In addition one must realize that the first word is used of all

[26]Text: PG, 83.757B-760A.
[27]Text: PG, 83.760C.

mothers, while the second one is proper to the virgin alone, and that this is the source of the whole quarrel, which, as far as we are concerned, should never have arisen at all. Most of the ancient fathers applied the more honorable title to the virgin, as you have done yourself in two are three discourses; I have seen several of these which you sent to me, and in them you have not joined the term "mother of a human being" to the title "mother of God," but have instead explained the meaning of the latter in different words.[28]

Letter 18: To Neoptolemus

11. When I consider the divine law which calls those who are united in marriage "one flesh" (see Gen. 2.24; Mt. 19.5-6; Mk. 10.8), I have no idea how to console the member left behind by the separation of death, for I am aware of the magnitude of the grief. But I do find many approaches to consolation when I think about the course of nature, about that decree which the creator passed with the words, "you are earth, and to earth you will return" (Gen. 3.19), and finally about what happens daily everywhere on land and sea—either husbands arrive first at the end of their lives, or wives are the first to suffer this. But in addition to these reflections I also think of the hopes bestowed on us by our God and savior; for here is why the mystery of God's plan [i.e., the incarnation] was accomplished: that we might learn that death had come to an end and not grieve too much when we were left alone through the death of those we love, but might await that longed for hope of the resurrection.[29]

Letter 21: To the Lawyer Eusebius

12. We believe, as we were taught, in one Father, Son, and holy Spirit. For even though certain liars have said it,

[28]Text: SC, 98, 58.
[29]Text: SC, 98, 64-66.

we have not been taught two sons, nor were we baptized into two sons, nor do we believe in, or teach anyone to believe in two sons. Just as we know one Father and one holy Spirit, so we know one Son, our lord Jesus Christ, the only begotten Son of God, God the Word who became human. For we do not deny the particular properties of the natures; but just as we think that those people are wicked who divide the one lord Jesus Christ into two sons, so we call enemies of the truth those people who attempt to blend the natures together. For we believe that the union took place without any blending, and we know that some properties belong to the humanity and others to the divinity.

The human being—and I am referring to the human being in general: the rational, mortal, living being—has a soul and a body, but is considered one living being; and the difference of the two natures does not divide the one [human being] into two persons. In the one being we know the immortality of the soul and the mortality of the body, and we acknowledge that the soul is invisible, while the body is visible, but that there is one living being, as I said, which is both rational and mortal. In the same way, we know that our lord and God, I mean the Son of God, the lord Christ, was one Son, even after becoming human. For the union admits of no division, just as it admits of no blending. And yet we know that the divinity has no beginning, while the humanity is more recent. For the latter springs from the seed of Abraham and David, since the holy virgin is descended from them; but the divine nature was begotten from God the Father before the ages, outside of time, without any change, and without any separation. If the distinction of the flesh and divinity were abolished, what weapons would we use in the battle against Arius and Eunomius? How could we crush their blasphemy against the only begotten? For our part, we apply the lowly words as to a human being, and the exalted and divine words as to God; and thus it is very easy for us to present the truth.[30]

[30]Text: SC, 98, 74-78.

Letter 25: Festal Letter

13. When the only begotten God became human, took our nature, and brought about our salvation, the people of that time, who actually saw the source of all blessings, did not celebrate a feast. But today, even though they cannot see their kind benefactor with their visible eyes, all the earth, the sea, cities, and villages celebrate a feast in memory of those blessings.[31]

Letter 38: Festal Letter

14. The divine feast of salvation has presented us with the springs of the gifts given by God: the blessing of the cross, the immortality, the resurrection which sprang from the death of the master, our lord Jesus Christ—that resurrection which promises the resurrection of all.[32]

Letter 63: Festal Letter

15. We have enjoyed as usual the delights of the feast. For we have celebrated the memorial of the sufferings that saved us. We have received, through the lord's resurrection, the good news of the resurrection of all, and we have sung of the ineffable love of our God and savior for us.[33]

Letter 64: Festal Letter

16. When the master went through the suffering that would save the human race, the choir of holy apostles was very sad, for they did not know clearly what the fruit of the suffering would be. But once they saw the salvation that sprang from it, they called the proclamation of the suffering good news, and eagerly offered it to all people. Those who believed because their minds were enlightened, received it with joy and celebrated the memorial feast of the suffer-

[31]Text: SC, 98, 82-84.
[32]Text: SC, 98, 102.
[33]Text: SC, 98, 142.

ing, making the time of his death an occasion of solemn festivity. For the resurrection is closely linked with his death and drives away sorrow at that death, becoming a pledge of the resurrection of all.[34]

Letter 76: To Uranius, Governor of Cyprus

17. You will clearly grasp with eagerness the gift given by God, encouraged by true friends who fully understand its value, and you will be led to the generous God, "Who wills that all people be saved and come to knowledge of the truth" (I Tim. 2.4); the same God, through other people, draws people into the net of salvation (see Mt. 4.19), bringing those who are captured into a life that never grows old. The fisherman takes life away from whatever he captures, but our fisherman frees the catch from the bitter chains of death. For this reason, [God] "appeared on the earth and associated with human beings" (Bar. 3.37 [LXX, 3.38]), and through the visible humanity, offered people the life-giving teaching, and legislated a way of life appropriate to rational beings. He confirmed these laws through miracles and destroyed death through the death of his flesh; he raised his flesh and promised all of us resurrection, by giving the resurrection of his own revered body as a worthy pledge of our resurrection. He so loved human beings— even those who hate what I have described—that the mystery of the divine plan is rejected by some because his sufferings were so horrible. And the fact that God continues daily to call those who disbelieve is enough to prove the depths of God's love for us. God does this, not because of a need for human service—what does the maker of everything lack?—but because God thirsts for the salvation of all.[35]

[34]Text: SC, 98, 144.
[35]Text: SC, 98, 164-166.

Letter 83: To Dioscorus, Bishop of Alexandria

18. I was forced to write this to you, as soon as I read your letters to bishop Domnus. For they said, among other things, that certain people had come to the great city you direct and had accused me of dividing our one lord Jesus Christ into two sons. I wept for those men, who dared to fabricate such a blatant lie; but I also grieved—please forgive me for saying this, but anguish forces me to speak—at the fact that you did not keep one ear open and unprejudiced for my side of the story, and instead believed the lies they told. I know that I am a pitiful creature, for I am guilty of many sins; but through faith alone I hope to enjoy some mercy on the day when God appears. For I desire to follow in the footsteps of the holy fathers and pray that I may do so; and I am eager to preserve in its purity the teaching of the gospel, which was delivered to us in summary form by the holy fathers who gathered at Nicaea in Bithynia.[36]

19. Just as I believe, therefore, in one God, Father, and in one holy Spirit who proceeds from the Father, so I believe in one lord Jesus Christ, only begotten Son of God, begotten from the Father before the ages, "radiance of the glory and image of the Father's reality" (Heb. 1.3), who, for the salvation of human beings, was made flesh and became human, and was born of Mary the virgin according to the flesh. Paul also taught us this: "To whom belong the patriarchs, and from whom is born, according to the flesh, the Christ, God who is over all, blessed forever. Amen" (Rom. 9.5). And he also said, "Concerning his Son who was born of the seed of David according to the flesh, and was designated Son of God in power according to the spirit of holiness" (Rom. 1.3-4). For this reason we also call the holy virgin mother of God, and consider those who reject this title to be people with no faith.[37]

20. As for those who divide our one lord Jesus Christ

[36]Text: SC, 98, 206-210.
[37]Text: SC, 98, 210-212.

into two persons, two sons, or two lords, we call them liars and expel them from the Christian community. The divine evangelist says, "And the Word became flesh and dwelt among us, and we have seen his glory, glory as of an only begotten from a father; and he is full of grace and truth" (Jn. 1.14). His namesake, the baptizer, says, "After me comes a man who was preferred before me, because he existed before me" (Jn. 1.30). After showing the one person, he affirmed both realities, the divine and the human; for "man" and "comes" refer to the human, while the words "because he existed before me" express the divine. And yet he knows that the one who comes after is not a different person from the one who exists before him, but realizes that this person is eternal as God, and also a human being born after him from the virgin. In the same way, Thomas put his hand in the lord's flesh and called him lord and God (Jn. 20.28), recognizing the invisible nature through the visible one. Thus we understand the difference between the flesh and the divinity, but we know that the divine Word who became human is one Son.[38]

21. [Earlier writers] teach us clearly the difference between the two natures and preach the unchanging character of the divine nature. They call the lord's flesh divine, since it became the flesh of God the Word; but they reject as wicked the idea that the flesh was transformed into the nature of the divinity. What I have written on holy scripture and against the Arians and Eunomians proves that I have expressed my true opinions here. In addition to this I am briefly adding one final point: If anyone does not say that the holy virgin is mother of God, or if anyone calls our lord Jesus Christ a mere human being, or divides into two sons the one only begotten and firstborn of all creation, let that person be excluded from the hope that comes through Christ; and may all the people say, "Amen, amen."[39]

[38]Text: SC, 98, 212-214.
[39]Text: SC, 98, 216-218.

Letter 146 (145): To the Monks of Constantinople

22. The church follows in the footsteps of the apostles and contemplates in the lord Christ both perfect divinity and perfect humanity. He took a body, not because he needed one, but to provide immortality to all bodies through his own; in the same way, he took the soul which rules the body, so that every soul might, through his, share in immutability. For even though souls are immortal, they are not immutable, but constantly undergo many changes, experiencing pleasure, first from one object, then from another. We go wrong, therefore, when we undergo change, and we tend toward things that are less good. But after the resurrection bodies enjoy immortality and incorruptibility, while souls enjoy freedom from passion and immutability. This is why the only begotten Son of God took a body and soul, preserved them free of all blame, and offered them as a sacrifice for the [human] race. He was, therefore, designated our high priest; but he was called high priest, not as God, but as a human being. As a human being, he makes the offering, but, as God, he receives the sacrifice, together with the Father and the holy Spirit. If only the body of Adam had sinned, then only the body would have needed a cure; but the body did not sin alone. The soul, in fact, sinned first, for thought first pictures the sin, and then carries it out through the body; it was, therefore, absolutely right for the soul also to obtain a cure.[40]

23. We have learned that the divine nature is immortal; for the part that could suffer did so, while the part that could not suffer remained free of suffering. God the Word became human, not to make the nature that could not suffer capable of suffering, but to give freedom from suffering, through his suffering, to the nature that could suffer.[41]

[40]Text: SC, 111, 182-184.
[41]Text: SC, 111, 186.

4. THE COUNCIL OF CHALCEDON[42]

All of us follow the holy fathers, therefore, and unanimously teach the confession of one and the same Son, our lord Jesus Christ, the same one perfect in divinity and the same one perfect in humanity; the same one, truly God and truly human, composed of a rational soul and body; of the same substance as the Father according to the divinity, and the same one of the same substance as us according to the humanity; like us in all things except sin; begotten from the Father before time according to the divinity, but in the last days the same one, for us and for our salvation, [begotten] from Mary the virgin, the mother of God, according to the humanity; one and the same Christ, Son, lord, only begotten, known in two natures, without mixture, change, division, or separation; the difference between the natures was in no way destroyed because of the union, but the proper quality of each nature is, rather, preserved and comes together [with the other] into one person and one existing individual; not divided or separated into two persons, but one and the same only begotten son, God, Word, lord, Jesus Christ, just as the prophets spoke about him from the beginning, as Jesus Christ himself taught us, and as the creed of the fathers has traditionally instructed us.

---

[42]This selection is the relevant part of the council's profession of faith. Text: *Conciliorum Oecumenicorum Decreta,* ed. Istituto per le scienze religiose (Bologna, 1973), pp. 86-87.

Suggested Reading

ANTHOLOGIES

Bettenson, Henry. *The Early Christian Fathers.* Oxford, 1956.

_____. *The Later Christian Fathers.* Oxford, 1970.

Carmody, James M. and Clarke, Thomas E. *Word and Redeemer.* Paulist Press, 1966.

Hardy, Edward R. *Christology of the Later Fathers.* Library of Christian Classics. The Westminster Press, 1954.

Norris, Richard A. *The Christological Controversy.* Sources of Early Christian Thought. Fortress Press, 1980.[1]

STUDIES

Beeck, Frans Josef van. *Christ Proclaimed.* Paulist Press, 1979.

Boff, Leonardo. *Jesus Christ Liberator: A Critical Christology for our Time.* Orbis Books, 1984.[2]

---

[1] This is the best of the recent anthologies that deal with the specific issue of Christology.

[2] This volume is written from the perspective of liberation theology.

Fuller, Reginald H. and Perkins, Pheme. *Who Is This Christ?* Fortress Press, 1983.

Grillmeier, Aloys. *Christ in Christian Tradition. Volume 1: From the Apostolic Age to Chalcedon (A.D. 451).* Second revised edition. Mowbrays, 1975.[3]

Kasper, Walter. *Jesus the Christ.* Paulist Press, 1977.

Küng, Hans. *On Being a Christian.* Doubleday, 1976.

Moule, C.F.D. *The Origin of Christology.* Cambridge U. Press, 1978.

O'Collins, Gerald. *What are they saying about Jesus?* Second edition. Paulist Press, 1983.

Ruether, Rosemary Radford. *Sexism and God-Talk: Toward A Feminist Theology.* Beacon Press, 1983.[4]

Sarkissian, Karekin. *The Council of Chalcedon and the Armenian Church.* The Armenian Church Prelacy, 1965.[5]

Schillebeeckx, Edward. *Jesus: An Experiment in Christology.* The Seabury Press, 1979.

_____. *Christ: The Experience of Jesus as Lord.* The Seabury Press, 1980.

Schüssler Fiorenza, Elisabeth. *Bread Not Stone: The Challenge of Feminist Biblical Interpretation.* Beacon Press, 1984.[6]

---

[3]This is the most comprehensive scholarly study of the subject matter in English.

[4]This volume offers material from a feminist viewpoint.

[5]This volume is written from the perspective of a church that does not accept the council of Chalcedon.

[6]This volume and the next offer material from a feminist viewpoint.

_____. *In Memory of Her.* The Crossroad Publishing Company, 1984.

Sellers, R.V. *The Council of Chalcedon.* S.P.C.K., 1953.

Sobrino, Jon. *Christology at the Crossroads.* Orbis Books, 1980.[7]

Tavard, George H. *Images of the Christ: An Enquiry into Christology.* University Press of America, 1982.

Wiles, Maurice. *The Christian Fathers.* SCM Press, 1977.

Winslow, Donald F. *The Dynamics of Salvation. A Study in Gregory of Nazianzus.* Patristic Monograph Series, No. 7. The Philadelphia Patristic Foundation, 1979.

Young, Frances. *From Nicaea to Chalcedon.* Fortress Press, 1983.

[7]This volume is written from the perspective of liberation theology.

Index

Since they appear on almost every page, divine names and titles, names of Old and New Testament figures, and common Christological, soteriological, and theological terms are not included. Adjectives based on proper nouns (e.g., Platonic, Plato) are listed under the noun.